What church leade

'I have been very encouraged to see the growth of use of Alpha courses.'

George Carey
Archbishop of Canterbury

'Alpha ... a clear way into Christian faith for a wide variety of people. I warmly and heartily commend the Alpha courses.'

David Hope
Archbishop of York

'Today God is using the Alpha course to bring thousands of unchurched people to himself. I rejoice to see Alpha spreading like wild fire, rekindling the passion for the perishing in the hearts of countless Christians. My prayer is that our churches will not bypass such a gift from God for our generation. I would strongly encourage churches to discover the exciting effectiveness of Alpha. New life, in more than one sense, begins with Alpha!'

Moses Tay
Archbishop of South East Asia

'I recognise the value of the Alpha course in helping people explore and strengthen their faith. I warmly commend it.'

Brian Davis
Archbishop of New Zealand

'This is what I understand Alpha to be about: to know about Jesus in order that I may know him and the power of his resurrection.'

Walter P. K. Makhulu
The Archbishop of Central Africa

'I am regularly commending the Alpha initiatives to parishes because I have seen the lasting growth and renewal where they have been used.'

Michael Turnbull
Bishop of Durham

'Real education ... Christian companionship ... a living experience of the mystery of God. I am so grateful for Alpha courses.'

Richard Chartres
Bishop of London

'What Alpha has to offer is a unique mixture of Christian content and Christian style. It isn't only about communicating what Christians believe; it communicates it in a way that becomes part of the message, showing how the teaching leads to a way of living, through friendship and hospitality. I recommend it to all the Christian family in these parts as a very special tool of evangelism.'

Rowan Williams
Bishop of Monmouth

'I have found the Alpha course compulsive reading. It is a very fine and compelling presentation of the Christian faith.'

Ambrose Griffiths, OSB
Bishop of Hexham and Newcastle Diocese

'The Alpha course is a most engaging way of passing on the basics of Christianity. It is a tool for evangelism and nurture that I highly recommend.'

J. I. Packer
Professor of Theology, Regent College, Vancouver

'Alpha courses are helping to change the face of the church in the UK. Throughout the country churches are catching on to a new and fresh approach to evangelism and the nurture of new believers. From small beginnings, Alpha is now making a major impact and providing the opportunity for churches of all denominations to adopt this significant model in obeying our Lord's command to "make disciples from every nation". I warmly commend the whole Alpha initiative.'

Clive Calver
General Director, Evangelical Alliance

'The Alpha course has now become one of the most reliable and important means of drawing people into the church and energising the faith of those who are already Christians. I strongly commend this to all church leaders and congregations who are looking for ways of expanding or consolidating their ministries. Although the approach was pioneered in London, England, it can easily be adapted to anywhere in the western hemisphere. It has enormous potential.'

Alister McGrath
Wycliffe Hall, Oxford and Regent College, Vancouver

'The Alpha course is to me another example of the ongoing need for each successive generation to express its faith in contemporary terms and on current issues. I am not surprised to hear of its immediate acceptance and use by hundreds of churches all over the world and, furthermore, of the consequent decisions for Christ that it has generated. More power to Jesus!'

John Wimber
Association of Vineyard Churches

'At the heart of the gospel is both evangelism and discipleship. Alpha courses are designed to do both effectively. We have used the programme in our local church with good success. I am glad to commend it.'

Gordon D. Fee
Professor of New Testament and Dean of Faculty, Regent College,
Vancouver, Canada

'For the first time I have seen a programme which embodies all of the principles which many of us involved in teaching evangelism have been expounding. I am delighted that the Alpha course is coming to North America. It is making an enormous impact in the UK, being acclaimed by churches of wide-ranging traditions, as well as submitted to scrutiny in evaluating the results. As our culture becomes increasingly secularised, the insights embodied in the Alpha course will be especially appropriate.'

Eddie Gibbs
Associate Rector for Discipleship

'God has used the Alpha ministry in a significant way to reach the seeking pre-Christians of England. We, in an increasingly secular-ised North America, have much we can learn from the Alpha leaders about the principles which have enabled them to reach a biblically illiterate generation. I warmly commend the leaders of these conferences and the information they will present.'

Leighton Ford
Leighton Ford Ministries

'The phenomenal growth of Alpha courses is showing the church that we do not need to be defensive about our faith, but can expect people to be interested, and then radically changed by the gospel.'

Elaine Storkey
The Institute for Contemporary Christianity

'Nothing is more apparent to me than the blessing of God on HTB and the Alpha course. It has crossed my mind that perhaps God wanted to put his seal on the Alpha course by making HTB the British fountainhead for the extraordinary blessing of the Holy Spirit on so many churches nowadays. If so, what greater endorsement can one want! In any case, the blessing of God is on the Alpha course and I praise God for it.'

Dr R. T. Kendall
Westminster Chapel

'Alpha courses are proving incredibly successful as an evangelistic format to reach people with the relevance of the gospel for our generation. The UK is being widely impacted by them and I would wholeheartedly encourage Christians in the USA to open their doors to the full impact of the ministry of Alpha.'

Terry Virgo
New Frontiers International

'I have met many unlikely people from different backgrounds who have been profoundly changed through attending this course.'

Jackie Pullinger
Hong Kong

'Alpha is an excellent introductory course for those who do not go to church or for whom an inherited Christianity has little meaning. I have no hesitation in recommending it to any church or group wishing to present the basic gospel message clearly and effectively.'

Charles Whitehead
International Catholic Charismatic Services

'Alpha has proved itself to be an effective way of exploring faith and deepening commitment to Jesus as Lord. I commend it warmly.'

Nigel McCulloch
Bishop of Wakefield, Chairman of the Decade of Evangelism

'One of the most encouraging developments in evangelism in the UK during the last few years has been the growth and obvious effectiveness of the Alpha group approach. It combines shape and purposefulness with great flexibility in use and we have seen it used in our diocese in churches of very different flavours. I am happy to commend it.'

Gavin Reid
Bishop of Maidstone

'I commend the Alpha courses because I know that many hundreds of our Baptist churches have found them very helpful – for introducing rank outsiders to the local church and reaching fringe members of the church and drawing them into the mainstream.'

John C. James
President, Baptist Union of Great Britain, 1996-7

'The Alpha course has been of enormous value to churches in strengthening fellowship and increasing effective evangelism in the local community.'

David Coffey
General Secretary, Baptist Union

'The Alpha course is a superbly produced tool which, if used prayerfully and systematically, could be revolutionary … The relaxed, non-threatening but crystal-clear presentations on the tapes could not fail to impact decisively both believer and enquirer alike. I am sold on Alpha and so is African Enterprise. We'll be using it and we hope you will too.'

Michael Cassidy
African Enterprise

'Every lively church needs a maternity ward! It needs a setting in which new Christians can be made and Christians can be made new. The Alpha course has proved itself to be a marvellous vehicle for this purpose, and it can be adapted to a very wide variety of cultures. In Britain it is proving to be one of the most effective evangelistic agencies at present, and it is something that any local church can run with proper training and encouragement.'

Michael Green and Michael Marshall
Advisors in Evangelism to the Archbishops of
Canterbury and York

'Alpha is the most effective and transferable introductory course to the Christian faith that I know.'

Steve Chalke
Oasis Trust

'Alpha seems especially blessed in that the Lord is using it to reach all sorts of people in all sorts of spiritual conditions.'

Luis Palau
Evangelist

'Alpha – not just the first letter of the Greek alphabet, but first choice for an illuminating perspective on Christianity. An ideal follow-up course for missions.'

J. John
Evangelist

'One of the most significant developments in evangelism in recent years and one of the most valuable resources for the church to emerge in the course of the Decade of Evangelism. Alpha is a proven, thoroughly tested, well researched, marvellously presented way of communicating the gospel in today's culture. It is being used to reach thousands of people with the heart of the Christian message.'

Canon Robert Warren
National Officer for Evangelism

'Alpha Courses have been successfully used among our Pioneer network of churches. They are an increasing resource to those wanting to see people find forgiveness and favour in God's eyes. The course is fun and unthreatening – just like our Lord himself!'

Gerald Coates
Director, Pioneer

'The Alpha course for the enquirer into the Christian faith, as well as for new Christians, is one of the most exciting, successful, and God-owned and blessed courses in our current decade. I recommend it without any reservations – we've seen it working in our own fellowship with great inspiration.'

Roger Forster
Ichthus Christian Fellowship

'Alpha is the most effective means of evangelism using small groups that I know. John Wesley's class meeting rediscovered.'

Rob Frost
National Evangelist, Methodist Church

'Alpha is easily the best Christian foundation course I know of. We found it exciting, easy to grasp and practical – *excellent!* I heartily endorse it.'

Paul Mercy
Assistant General Superintendent, Assemblies of God

'Alpha … is based on the local church, sees evangelism as a process which involves the whole of a person, and has much to say about the power and work of the Holy Spirit in the church's evangelistic outreach. I am happy to commend it, and trust that many individuals and churches will find increasing help with the Alpha courses.'

Donald English
General Secretary, Methodist Home Mission Division

'A growing number of parishes are conducting Alpha courses and I have seen for myself how dramatically and excitingly these courses are bearing fruit. They are bringing people into a living and active faith, and I strongly commend them.'

Simon Barrington-Ward
Bishop of Coventry

'Alpha is a soul winning, discipling, multiplying, spiritually dynamic ministry that has already touched the lives of thousands. I believe this vision will continue to expand and truly become an international blessing.'

Loren Cunningham
Youth With A Mission International

'I am very pleased to write about the Alpha course. We live in a time when the majority of the population knows little or nothing of Christian beliefs or Christian values. The great strength of the Alpha course is that it allows genuine enquirers to take time in exploring Christian beliefs and Christian values, while building relationships with members of the church. God is using this course to lead many people to faith in Christ, to active membership of his church and to know the power of the Holy Spirit. I warmly commend it.'

Graham Cray
Principal of Ridley Hall, Cambridge

'I have been thrilled at the natural, winsome way Alpha has reached people, not least in my own family.'

John Goldingay
Principal, St John's College, Nottingham

'Alpha courses are not only bringing many new people to faith in Jesus Christ, but revitalising the lives of church members, who are discovering the limitless resources of the Holy Spirit. The Alpha course is thoroughly practical, earthed to many of the key issues that all of us face. I see it as one of the most significant ways in which God is bringing fresh dynamism and vision to the church.'

John Perry
Bishop of Southampton

'Alpha allows the doubters to doubt and the seekers to find the truth. It provides an enjoyable and supportive atmosphere in which to tackle the great questions of life.'

Graham Dow
Bishop of Willesden

'The Alpha courses, with their emphasis on the basics of the Christian faith, are meeting the needs of many who are currently searching for meaning in life.'

Roy Warke
Bishop of Cork, Cloyne and Ross

'The Alpha courses are being used extensively in this diocese and are proving to be an effective means of evangelism here in both urban and suburban areas. The user-friendly style is transforming many congregations and their approach to outreach.'

Michael Dickens Whinney
Assistant Bishop, Diocese of Birmingham

'I am very impressed with the Alpha programme and with the evangelistic breakthroughs that you get with Alpha courses.'

Moss Ntlah
Concerned Evangelicals, South Africa

'I highly recommend the Alpha course to everyone interested in discovering how the Christian faith can be exciting and life-changing in the modern world. The course is biblically sound, understandable, and practical. It will have a significant impact on people's lives and it will strengthen every church in which it is held.'

Wayne Grudem
Professor of Biblical and Systematic Theology,
Trinity International University, Deerfield, Illinois

'My Anglican friends in England are very enthusiastic about the Alpha conference. At a time when many are seeking spiritual formation in the context of congregational life, the Alpha conference format has the potential to meet those expectations.'

Ronald H. Haines
Bishop of Washington

'The Alpha courses are transforming churches all across Britain, showing extraordinary success in stimulating interest ... and then real faith among the uninterested and unchurched. I am so pleased to learn the courses are being introduced to the American and Canadian churches as well. A must for anyone serious about bringing others to Christ.'

John W. Howe
Bishop of Central Florida

'I welcome the introduction of the Alpha conferences into the church in the United States. These conferences combine sound teaching, personal experience of Christian community, and commitment to life in the faith and will be a welcome addition to the process of renewing the church.'

Peter James Lee
Bishop of Virginia

'...this course's beginning is orientated towards warming the faith of baptised people and then goes beyond that to the unbaptised. If Alpha does for us what it has done in other places, we are richly blessed.'

Richard F. Grein
Bishop of New York

'Nicky Gumbel loves Christ, is a student of the Word and has a passion for the things that Christ had on his heart ... the lost and his people.'

Paul Stanley
Vice President, The Navigators

'Alpha has pioneered a way of doing evangelism in which people are exposed both to the truths of the gospel and the power of the Spirit. Here at last is a means of communicating the gospel which does not divorce Word and Spirit.'

Mark Stibbe
Vicar of St Andrew's, Chorleywood

'The great command to make disciples of all people is still relevant. Alpha provides us with contemporary cringe-free evangelism which deserves the increasing profile it is currently receiving.'

Joel Edwards
Director of UK Development, Evangelical Alliance

'In our task of sharing the gospel as it is, with people where they are, Alpha is a creative and contemporary means of successfully doing this. I love it and think it is inspired!'

Lyndon Bowring
Executive Chairman of CARE

'Alpha, as developed by Nicky Gumbel and the leaders of HTB, employs all the best principles for effective evangelism – that is why it is so fruitful.'

Lynn Green
Director of Europe, Middle East and Africa Department, YWAM

'One of the most significant evangelistic enterprises since Billy Graham in the 1950s.'

David Pytches
Former Vicar of St Andrew's, Chorleywood

'The Alpha course is one of the most exciting evangelistic initiatives that has come to the church in this decade. Don't miss it!'

Rob Parsons
Executive Director, Care for the Family

'There is nothing like Alpha! Our prayer is that it will be discovered by many other churches throughout the world.'

John and Christine Noble
Pioneer

'I am quite certain that Alpha is crucial to evangelism in this country: it is Bible-centred, adaptable across traditions and denominations and above all answers the two most important yearnings that Springboard has found as it has gone around the UK – for basic teaching in the gospel and for a deeper spirituality.

It is tremendously adaptable and I know of its uses in Roman and Anglo-Catholic churches, as well as in Pentecostal and Baptist churches. It is also adaptable in terms of numbers. Springboard's experience is that Alpha is at the cutting edge of evangelism in this country at the moment.'

Martin Cavender
Administrative Director of 'Springboard', an initiative of the Archbishops of Canterbury and York for the Decade of Evangelism

'Alpha is fast proving to be an important part of the ministry through the church, especially these days when there is so much doubt and uncertainty in the minds of many people, even believers.'

Z. W. Gill
Bishop for the Kimberley and Bloemfontein District, South Africa

'Alpha brings together so many aspects of what God is doing today; it is a tool of our time.'

Ken Gott
Sunderland Christian Centre (Assemblies of God)

'One of the most effective tools of evangelism in the body of Christ in the United Kingdom is the Alpha course. This new and effective course has exploded, being used by hundreds of churches resulting in thousands of new believers being integrated into the local church. The enthusiasm is spreading rapidly. I wholeheartedly recommend Nicky Gumbel's excellent leadership. God has blessed the church greatly in raising up Nicky to trumpet the Alpha course.'

Mike Bickle
Metro Vineyard Fellowship, Kansas City

Telling Others

The Alpha Initiative

Nicky Gumbel

KINGSWAY PUBLICATIONS
EASTBOURNE

Co-published in South Africa with SCB Publishers
Cornelis Struik House, 80 McKenzie Street
Cape Town 8001, South Africa.
Reg no 04/02203/06

Front cover illustration and text cartoons by
Charlie Mackesy.

ISBN 0 85476 741 X

Designed and produced by Bookprint Creative Services
P.O. Box 827, BN21 3YJ, England, for
KINGSWAY PUBLICATIONS LTD
Lottbridge Drove, Eastbourne, E Sussex BN23 6NT.
Printed in Great Britain.

Contents

Foreword

As we look around at the state of the church, the figures of declining congregations, the crumbling buildings, the general sense of failure that haunts so much of the body of Jesus Christ today, there is a temptation for many of us involved in Christian ministry to feel discouraged. St Paul faced the same situation, yet he was able to say, 'Therefore, since through God's mercy we have this ministry, we do not lose heart' (2 Cor 4:1).

It isn't that people are not interested in spirituality – interest in the occult, religious experiences, spiritism, and other related forms of alternative searches is as great today as ever it was – but the universal spiritual hunger, that need to fill the God-shaped hole, has not been met by those things. Our experience at Holy Trinity Brompton has been that people are now showing a new interest in the claims of Jesus Christ and the Christian faith. As our society moves into a post-Christian era many who are ignorant of the basic claimed truth of Christianity are wanting to find out more about Jesus of Nazareth, especially if they can be sure of an atmosphere of acceptance, without feeling threatened, judged or made to look foolish. That is one of the reasons why I think the Alpha course has proved to be such a success. The issues are clearly put and the claims of Christ examined, all in the company of other searchers and in an atmosphere of love and acceptance.

Nicky Gumbel inherited Alpha several years ago and, since then, by taking account of literally thousands of questionnaires, has adapted and improved the course so it is truly moulded to the perceived and experienced needs of those who attend. Without taking anything for granted, stripping the gospel down to its bare essentials, he has made Christianity accessible to this generation.

But it is not simply hard work which has brought about the growth of Alpha. The touch of the Holy Spirit has brought the course to life from beginning to end. Hunger is created, in the hearts of those who are taking part, for the reality of God. The Spirit alone can satisfy them. By revealing the reality of the power of Jesus Christ to forgive, to release, empower and equip, new life begins for so many who are in need of God.

At the time of going to print, there are currently hundreds of Alpha courses running throughout this country and in other parts of the world. They range from small groups of five people to larger courses like one that is running here at Holy Trinity at the moment, with over five hundred people attending.

I know that you will enjoy this book. I am confident too that by God's grace you will find many people coming into the kingdom as a result of putting into practice the principles here.

Sandy Millar
Vicar of Holy Trinity Brompton

Preface

Thousands of people around the world are now taking part in Alpha courses – a ten week practical introduction to the Christian faith, designed primarily for non-churchgoers and those who have recently become Christians. In May 1993 we hosted a conference at Holy Trinity Brompton for church leaders who wanted to run such courses. Over a thousand people came, and hundreds of Alpha courses began all over the UK as a result. Since then we have held a number of regional conferences and have also been invited to do some international conferences. The number of Alpha courses in operation is growing daily.

This book is intended primarily to be a resource for churches who wish to run an Alpha course, although many of the principles of evangelism will have a wider application.

Alpha has evolved from what was essentially a basic introduction for new Christians to something which is aimed primarily at those outside the church. It was started at Holy Trinity Brompton in 1977 by Anglican clergyman Charles Marnham as a four-week course for new Christians. John Irvine took it over in 1981; he lengthened it to ten weeks and added a weekend for teaching on the person and work of the Holy Spirit. When Nicky Lee took it over in 1985 there were about thirty-five people on each course and under his leadership that grew to well over a hundred. Since then it has grown again to over five hundred people (including the leadership team) on each course (three a year). It seems sensible to pass on some of the things we have learned over the years.

In addition to the theological principles and the practical details of how courses are run, each alternate chapter consists of a testimony of someone whose life has been changed by God through an Alpha course. Each person writes in their own individual style, having recorded their experiences while the events were still fresh in their memory. Nigel Skelsey's story is taken from a letter he wrote days after his conversion to Christ. The others are based on interviews given to Mark Elsdon-Dew and originally published in *Focus* newspaper of which he is the editor. He has kindly allowed me to include this material in the book.

Most of my experience of the course has been with the evening Alpha course at Holy Trinity Brompton; in Appendix C I have included an account by Deidre Hurst on her experience of running a daytime Alpha.

I would like to express my thanks to Jon Soper who has acted as a researcher for this and all the other Alpha resource books. I am so grateful for his thoroughness, speed and efficiency as well as his very perceptive comments and suggestions.

I am grateful to all the people who have read the manuscripts and offered their valuable insights and criticisms. I want to thank especially Jo Glen, Patricia Hall, Helena Hird, Simon Levell, Ken Costa, Tamsen Carter, the Revd Alex Welby, Judy Cahusac, Nicola Hinson, Chris Russell and Simon Downham.

Finally, a big thank you to Philippa Pearson Miles for her chapter on Administration and for typing the manuscript and organising the project with her extraordinary combination of speed and enthusiasm, together with calmness and patience.

1
Principles

I have never been a natural evangelist. I have never found it easy to talk to my friends about Jesus Christ. Some people are completely natural evangelists; they find it the easiest thing in the world. I recently heard about one man who seizes every opportunity to talk to people about Jesus. If he is standing at a bus stop and the bus is late, he turns that situation into a conversation about the Second Coming! I have another friend who is a tremendously confident evangelist and speaks about Jesus wherever he goes. On a train he will speak to the person opposite about Jesus. If he's walking along the street he will turn to someone and get into conversation with them about Jesus. When he and his family go to a Happy Eater, upon finishing his meal, he bangs the table and calls for silence in the restaurant. He then stands up and preaches the gospel for five minutes. He says that at the end people come up to him and say, 'Thank you very much, that was very helpful.' I couldn't do that.

I first became a Christian just over twenty years ago. I was so excited about what had happened that I longed for everybody to follow suit. After I had been a Christian for only a few days I went to a party, determined to tell everyone. I saw a friend dancing and decided the first step was to make her realise her need. So I went up to her and said, 'You look awful. You really need Jesus.' She

thought I had gone mad. It was not the most effective
way of telling someone the good news. (However, she
did later become a Christian, quite independently of me,
and she is now my wife!)

If we charge around like a bull in a china shop, sooner
or later we will get hurt. Even if we approach the subject
sensitively, we may still get hurt. When we do, we tend
to withdraw. Certainly this was my experience. After a
few years, I moved from the danger of insensitivity and
fell into the opposite danger of fear. There was a time
(ironically when I was at theological college) when I
became fearful of even talking about Jesus to those who
were not Christians. On one occasion, a group of us went
from college to a parish mission on the outskirts of
Liverpool, to tell people the good news. Each night we
had supper with different people from the parish. One
night a friend of mine called Rupert and I were sent to a
couple who were on the fringe of the church (or to be
more accurate, the wife was on the fringe and the
husband was not a churchgoer). Halfway through the
main course the husband asked me what we were doing
up there. I stumbled, stammered, hesitated and prevari-
cated. He kept repeating the question. Eventually Rupert
said straight out, 'We have come here to tell people about
Jesus.' I felt deeply embarrassed and hoped the ground
would swallow us all up! I realised how frozen with fear
I had become and that I was afraid even to take the name
of Jesus on my lips.

Ever since then I've been looking for ways in which
ordinary people like me, who aren't naturally gifted
evangelists, can communicate their faith with friends,
family and colleagues without feeling fearful or risking
insensitivity. I have found that Alpha is evangelism for
ordinary people.

Recent surveys have shown that approximately a
thousand people left the Church of England every week

during the decade 1980 to 1990. Other denominations suffered a similar decline. The vast majority of the population of the United Kingdom do not attend church, and of those who do, many only go at Christmas or Easter. Following in the wake of the decline in Christian belief, there has been a decline in the moral climate. The fabric of our society is unravelling. Every day in Britain at least 480 couples are divorced, 170 babies are born to teenage mothers and 470 babies are aborted. In addition, at least one new crime is committed every six seconds and a violent attack takes place every two minutes. Although there are 30,000 Christian clergy of all types, there are more than 80,000 registered witches and fortune tellers.[1]

But at the same time, shoots of new life are springing up all over the place. New churches are being planted and many churches are seeing growth, sometimes slow and sometimes quite dramatic. There are new Christian initiatives arising out of the renewal movement in the Decade of Evangelism. One of those new shoots is the Alpha course. All of us involved with it have sensed the extraordinary blessing of God upon it.

I realise that we need to be cautious about saying this is a work of God. I know the story of the man who came up to a preacher and said, 'That was a great talk.' The preacher rather piously replied, 'It wasn't me, it was the Lord,' to which the man replied, 'It wasn't that good!' In saying that we believe Alpha is a work of God I am not for a moment suggesting that it is perfect. I'm sure that it is greatly marred by human error and frailty. There is much room for improvement and we try to listen carefully to constructive criticism. Nor do we believe that it is the only method of evangelism that God is blessing: far from it. Nevertheless, all the signs point to it being an extraordinary work of God and we are deeply grateful.

When Alpha first started growing I thought, 'How

could something that started in Central London work elsewhere?' Alpha currently runs in more than fifty countries: in Zimbabwe, Kenya, Norway, Denmark, Sweden, Germany, Malaysia, Hong Kong, Australia, New Zealand, the United States, Canada and many others.

While at an Alpha conference in Zimbabwe recently, I discovered that Alpha was not only running among the English-speaking white Zimbabweans but also among the Shona-speaking people in their own language. Zimbabwe has a population of just over 10 million people: there are 80,000 whites in Zimbabwe but 90% of the black population speak Shona. While I was at the conference I met a man called Edward Ngamuda. He had originally done Alpha in English but then thought that he would like to run the course in Shona. A couple who had come to Christ on Alpha asked him to come and run the course with the 900 people who worked on their farm. Thirty people came on the first course and fifty came on the second. I asked him whether these people were Christians when they came on the course. 'No,' he replied, 'we had a Muslim, a witchdoctor and a polygamist come.' I asked how the polygamist happened to be there and was told that his first wife came on the first course, and that she had brought him and the other two wives on the next one! Edward assured me that Alpha worked better in Shona than it did in English. It was then that I began to realise that this course, which started in London, could operate in different countries and cultures. Why is this?

I believe it is because Alpha is based on six New Testament principles; in this first chapter, I want to look at each of these principles in turn.

Evangelism[2] is most effective through the local church

John Stott, author of many books and Rector Emeritus of

All Souls, Langham Place, has described evangelism through the local church as 'the most normal, natural and productive method of spreading the gospel today'.[3] There are at least four reasons for this.

What you see is what you get

Missions and Billy Graham-style crusades clearly have been greatly used by God. They raise the profile of the church and are still an effective means of bringing people to Christ. In our church we often take teams on missions to universities and elsewhere and we appreciate the value and fruitfulness of this type of evangelism. But missions are more likely to bear lasting fruit if they are earthed in an ongoing programme of local church evangelism, because they then have the great advantage of continuity of relationships. Someone may respond at a crusade or mission and be referred to their local church. They may be disappointed to find the environment of the church radically different from the meeting which attracted them in the first place and so they subsequently stop attending. This is one of the reasons why the follow-up after big crusades is so hard. By contrast, if someone is introduced to Christianity at their local church, they become familiar with the place and the people, and are therefore much more likely to stay. We are finding on Alpha that belonging comes before believing for many people.

It mobilises a whole army of evangelists

In every church there are people who have gifts which can be used in evangelism but often their gifts are not recognised. For example, a Gallup survey discovered that only 10% of American church members are active in any kind of personal ministry. However, an additional 40% expressed an interest in having a ministry, but did not know how to start.

This group is an untapped gold mine. On every Alpha course, approximately one third of the people involved are leaders and helpers, all of them doing evangelism. Tens of thousands of people are now involved. Steve Morgan, the Rural Dean of Merthyr Tydfil in South Wales, put it like this:

> It has been the heart cry of past generations to put evangelism within the grasp of ordinary people who are terrified at the thought of evangelism. This has never happened before. We have here 'a history-making-thing'. For generations, the only people who would touch evangelism were those with an outgoing personality. But now the shy little old lady can embrace evangelism for the first time. It has never been available for all types of personality before. Any church, at any time, with any group can run with this. We believe that the nation has been praying, and calling out for this, for generations.

It is friendship based

Alpha is a New Testament model of evangelism: Peter brought his brother Andrew; Philip brought his friend Nathaniel; the woman at the well went back and told everyone in her town; and Matthew the tax collector threw a party and invited all his work colleagues to meet Jesus.

The pattern on Alpha is that people come to Christ and are filled with the Spirit. They then realise the wonder, the importance, and the relevance of what God has done for them through Christ and they want to tell their friends, family and work colleagues. Most of these others probably do not go to church nor are they Christians. These in turn come and do the course. Some of them come to Christ, and are filled with the Spirit. They too become excited about Jesus and tell *their* friends, family and colleagues. In this way we find that we are constantly breaking into new circles of unchurched people.

The more checkouts, the more customers

One crusade may bring great blessing but it is limited both in time and space. If every local church in the world was running an effective ongoing programme of local church evangelism and every month people were coming to Christ and bringing their friends and these friends bringing other friends – imagine how quickly the world would be reached for Christ!

Michael Green, Advisor in Evangelism to the Archbishops of Canterbury and York, in his book *Evangelism through the Local Church*, summed up the need for this kind of evangelism:

> Whenever Christianity has been at its most healthy, evangelism has stemmed from the local church, and has had a noticeable impact on the surrounding area. I do not believe that the re-Christianisation of the West can take place without the renewal of local churches in this whole area of evangelism. We need a thoughtful, sustained, relevant presentation of the Christian faith, in word and in action, embodied in a warm, prayerful, lively local church which has a real concern for its community at all levels.... Such evangelism, in and from the local church, is not only much needed but … eminently possible. I believe it to be the most natural, long-lasting and effective evangelism that is open to us. If local churches were engaging in loving, outgoing evangelism within their neighbourhoods, many of our evangelistic campaigns, missions and crusades would be rendered much less necessary.[4]

Evangelism is a process

Conversion may take place in a moment but it is part of a process. Jesus used the expression 'born again' (Jn 3:3) for the beginning of a spiritual life, and the New Testament speaks about becoming a child of God. While the birth of a child may be one event, there is a much longer process before and afterwards. The Bible uses many other images to represent spiritual growth: some are taken from agriculture, others from the ideas of building or journeying. All these involve a process.

Alpha is a ten-week course involving a total of fifteen talks which include a weekend and a celebration party at the end. We do not expect people to respond to the gospel after the first week (although some do). We recognise that people need time to think, watch, listen, and to talk through their questions and difficulties. Each person is beginning at a different stage.

Some are already Christians but will often say, in retrospect, that at the start of the course they were Christians 'without any real experience of God'. Others are at the point of new birth when they begin Alpha. Some have already given their lives to Christ at the party at the end of the previous course, others at a guest service before the beginning of Alpha. Still others perhaps come to faith through the witness of their family or a friend. Many are still a long way off when they begin Alpha. Some are convinced atheists, some are New Agers, some are adherents to other religions or cults. Many are living in lifestyles which are far from Christian. Some are alcoholics, others are compulsive gamblers, many are living with partners to whom they are not married and some are in a homosexual lifestyle. We welcome them all. Some will complete the whole course and still not be Christians at the end; we hope they will be unable to say they have not heard the gospel. Others will give their lives to Christ somewhere on the course. For nearly all of them, Alpha will enable them to take a step forward in their relationship with God.

The fact there is a process spread over fifteen sessions enables us to give longer to aspects of the Christian faith than one would be able to in one evangelistic talk. For example, in 1994 I saw a man standing at the back of the room who looked very suspicious and worried. When I introduced myself he said, 'I don't want to be here, I've been dragged along.' I said, 'Great! Let me introduce you to eleven other people who don't want to be here,' and I took him to meet my small group. At the end of the evening I heard him chatting to someone else in the group.

'Are you coming back next week?'

The other man replied, 'Yes, I'll be here.'

To which the first man said, 'Well, if you're coming back next week, I'll come back next week.'

Six weeks later he said to me, 'This course is like a jigsaw puzzle. Every time I come back another piece fits into place. And I'm beginning to get the picture.'

Furthermore, the fact that Alpha is a process enables trust to develop. There is a great deal of cynicism, scepticism, and distrust about the Christian church. I had no idea of the extent of this until I spoke to someone who said that for the first three weeks of the course he had not eaten the food in case it was drugged. That was an extreme case of distrust but many people wonder if the church is after their money, their mind or something else. It can take a few weeks for a level of trust to build. As the guests get to know their small group leaders, they begin to see that they are not 'after' anything and they start to listen.

Evangelism involves the whole person

Evangelism involves an appeal to the whole person: mind, heart and will. Each talk is designed to appeal to all three, although in some of the talks the emphasis will be on just one.

We appeal to the mind because we believe that Christianity is based in history: on the life, death and resurrection of Jesus Christ. We preach 'Jesus Christ and him crucified' (1 Cor 2:2). We seek to persuade with every argument we can muster, just as Paul did on so many occasions (eg Acts 18:4). We try to teach only what we can establish from the Bible and we point people to the biblical text. We do not expect anyone to take a 'blind leap' of faith. Rather, we hope they will take a step of faith based on reasonable grounds.

Secondly, we appeal to the heart. Our message does not simply require an assent of the intellect to a series of propositions, rather it calls people to a love-relationship with Jesus Christ. John Stott has written:

> There is a place for emotion in spiritual experience. The Holy Spirit's … ministry is not limited to illuminating our minds and teaching us about Christ. He also pours God's love into our hearts. Similarly, he bears witness with our spirit that we are God's children, for he causes us to say 'Abba, father' and to exclaim with gratitude, 'How great is the love the father has lavished on us, that we should be called children of God!' … I think it was Bishop Handley Moule at the end of the last century who gave this good advice: 'Beware equally of an undevotional theology (ie mind without heart) and of an untheological devotion (ie heart without mind).[5]

Graham Cray, principal of Ridley Hall theological college in Cambridge, has spoken with great insight about the culture of the 1990s, which is in the process of shifting from an Enlightenment culture to a new and coming one. In the Enlightenment, reason reigned supreme and explanation led to experience. In the present transitional culture with its 'pick-and-mix' worldview, in which the New Age movement is a potent strand, experiences lead to explanation.

I have found on Alpha that those from an essentially Enlightenment background feel at home with the parts of the course which appeal to the mind, but often have difficulty in experiencing the Holy Spirit. Others coming from the New Age movement find that rational and historical explanations leave them cold, but at the weekend away they are on more familiar territory in experiencing the Spirit. Previously they will have been seeking experiences which have then left them discontented and only in experiencing a relationship with God through Jesus Christ do they find their hunger is satisfied.

The gospel involves both the rational and the experiential and it impacts both those from an Enlightenment background who need to experience God and those who have sought experiences but who need to understand the truth about God.

Thirdly, we seek to appeal to the will. We recognise, of course, that no one can come to the Father unless God calls them. As Jesus said, 'No-one knows the Son except the Father, and no-one knows the Father except the Son and those to whom the Son chooses to reveal him' (Mt 11:27). On the other hand, Jesus went on to say in the very next verse, 'Come to me, all you who are weary and burdened, and I will give you rest' (Mt 11:28). In other words, he called for a decision.

There is a difference between an appeal to the will and

the wrong form of pressure. We try to avoid all forms of pressure on Alpha. We do not endlessly exhort anyone to respond, or chase people up if they do not come back: it is up to them to decide. Over the period of ten weeks, as we pray and allow the Holy Spirit to do his work, giving people the opportunity to respond, we are, in effect, making a continuous appeal to their wills.

Models of evangelism in the New Testament include classical, holistic and power evangelism

Graham Tomlin, lecturer at Wycliffe Hall Theological College, Oxford, draws attention to three different models of evangelism.[6] Clearly these three are not mutually exclusive and we very much hope that the Alpha course involves all three models.

Classical evangelism – words

First, there is *classical evangelism* which involves 'the proclamation of the unchanging message'. Certainly, at the heart of Alpha is the proclamation of the gospel of Jesus Christ: the first talk is about Christ's deity, the second is about his death on the cross for us and each talk has at its core some principle of Christian belief and living.

We do not believe we have the liberty to tamper with the apostolic message. However, the message comes to us in a cultural packaging. Every generation has a duty to ensure that the packaging is not a stumbling block; to preserve the unchanging message but to change the packaging in order to make it understandable in the context of our own culture. Martin Luther translated the Scriptures into the German vernacular, and the Lutheran church adapted the folk music of the day into songs of worship. The Methodist church under the leadership of the Wesley brothers were 'agreed to become more vile to reach the common people and to speak in the most obvious, easy, common words, wherever our meaning can be conveyed'. General William Booth, the founder of the Salvation Army, memorably said, 'Why should the devil have all the good tunes?'

Holistic evangelism – works

Secondly, there is *holistic evangelism*. As John Stott wrote, 'We are convinced that God has given us social as well as evangelistic responsibilities in his world.'[7]

Evangelism and social action go hand in hand. The latter involves both social justice in the removal of injustice, inhumanity and inequality and social service in relieving human need, such as hunger, homelessness and poverty. We attempt on Alpha to avoid the dangers of pietism by our teaching and example, believing that evangelism is fundamentally linked to social responsibility.

As Bishop Lesslie Newbigin puts it, 'The life of the worshipping congregation, severed from its proper expression in compassionate service to the secular community around it, risks becoming a self-centred existence serving only the needs and desires of its members.'[8]

Power evangelism – wonders

Thirdly, there is *power evangelism*, where the proclamation of the gospel goes hand in hand with a demonstration of the Spirit's power (1 Cor 2:1-5). We include this third element because we believe it is firmly based in New Testament practice.

It used to be argued that you cannot take doctrine from narrative, but New Testament scholars have shown to the satisfaction of theologians of all varieties that the gospel writers were not only historians, they were theologians as well. In a different literary form, they were writing theology as much as Paul or the other writers of the New Testament epistles. In the gospels, the central theme in the teaching of Jesus is the kingdom of God.[8] The coming of the kingdom involved not only the spoken proclamation of the gospel but also a visible demonstration of its presence by signs, wonders and miracles. Each of the gospel writers expected these to continue.

We can see this from the way in which Matthew sets out his Gospel. He tells us that 'Jesus went throughout Galilee, teaching in their synagogues, preaching the good news of the kingdom, and healing every disease and sickness among the people' (Mt 4:23). He then gives some of the teaching and preaching of Jesus in chapters 5-7 (the Sermon on the Mount), then nine miracles (mainly of healing) and he concludes with an almost exact repetition of Matthew 4: 23: 'Jesus went through all the towns and villages, teaching in their synagogues, preaching the good news of the kingdom and healing every disease and sickness' (Mt 9: 35). Matthew is using a literary device of repetition known as an 'inclusio', a short piece of text which appears at the beginning and at the end of a particular section and which acts as punctuation by enclosing a theme. Having shown what Jesus himself did, Matthew tells us that Jesus then sent the twelve out to do the same. He told them to go out and preach the same message: '"The kingdom of heaven is near." Heal the sick, raise the dead, cleanse those who have leprosy, drive out demons…' (Mt 10: 7-8).

At the end of his Gospel, Matthew makes it clear that Jesus expected all his disciples to 'go and make disciples of all nations...teaching them to obey *everything* I have commanded you' (Mt 28: 19-20, italics mine). This surely includes not only his ethical teaching, but also the earlier commissions.

In Mark's Gospel we see a similar pattern. Mark tells us that Jesus proclaimed the good news (Mk 1:14

onwards) demonstrating it by signs and wonders (Mk 1:21 onwards). The kingdom of God was inaugurated by Jesus and is still growing to this day. There is no reason why its fundamental nature should have changed. Indeed, in the longer ending of Mark (which is, at the very least, good evidence of what the early church believed Jesus' commission to be) Jesus said, '"Go into all the world and preach the good news to all creation … and these signs will accompany *those who believe*: In my name they will drive out demons … they will place their hands on sick people, and they will get well.…" Then the disciples went out and preached everywhere, and the Lord worked with them and confirmed his word by the signs that accompanied it' (Mk 16:15-20, italics mine). Jesus says, 'These signs will accompany *those who believe*' – that is to say, those who believe in Jesus Christ, which means all Christians.

For Luke's theology we need to look at both Luke and Acts. Luke tells us in his Gospel: 'When Jesus had called the Twelve together, he gave them power and authority to drive out all demons and to cure diseases, and he sent them out to preach the kingdom of God and to heal the sick' (Lk 9:1-2). Nor was it only the Twelve to whom he gave this commission; he also appointed seventy-two others and told them to go out and 'heal the sick who are there and tell them, "The kingdom of God is near you"' (Lk 10:9).

In the book of Acts this continues beyond the time Jesus was on earth. After the outpouring of the Holy Spirit, there is a remarkable continuation of supernatural power, ranging from speaking in tongues to raising the dead. These demonstrations of power continue right through to the last chapter (Acts 28:7-9). In the Acts of the Apostles we see the outworking of this commission. The disciples continued to preach and teach, but also to heal the sick, raise the dead and cast out demons (Acts

3:1-10; 4:12; 5:12-16; 8:5-13; 9:32-43; 14:3, 8-10; 19:11-12; 20:9-12; 28:8-9).

Nor is this ministry in the Spirit's power confined to the synoptic gospels. In John's Gospel Jesus is reported to have said, in the context of miracles, 'Anyone who has faith in me will do what I have been doing. He will do even greater things than these, because I am going to the Father' (Jn 14:12). Clearly no one has performed miracles of greater quality than Jesus, but there has been a greater quantity since Jesus returned to the Father. He has not ceased to perform miracles, but now he uses weak and imperfect human beings. Again it says, 'Anyone who has faith in me': that is, all Christians. These commands and promises are not restricted anywhere to a special category of people.

Signs and miracles were a central part of Paul's proclamation of the gospel (Rom 15:19). It is also clear from 1 Corinthians 12-14 that Paul did not believe that such abilities were confined to the apostles and he expected the more obviously supernatural gifts of the Spirit to continue in an effective and healthy church. He speaks about 'gifts of healing', 'miraculous powers', 'prophecy', 'speaking in different kinds of tongues' and 'the interpretation of tongues'. He described these as being given to different members of the body of Christ and as being the work of the Spirit (1 Cor 12:7-11).

Nowhere in the New Testament does it say that these gifts will cease at the end of the apostolic age. On the contrary, Paul says that they will only cease when 'perfection comes' (1 Cor 13:10). Some have identified 'perfection' here with the formation of the canon of Scripture, saying that as we now have the Bible, we have no need of 'imperfect' spiritual gifts. However, the context for this verse clearly shows that Paul is identifying 'perfection' with the return of Jesus. The world is not yet perfect, neither do we see Jesus 'face to face' (v 12), nor do we 'know fully' (v 12) but we know only 'in part' (v 12). This 'perfection' will only occur when Jesus returns and then these gifts will no longer be necessary. Until that moment they are a vital part of the church's armoury. Indeed, this passage shows that Paul did not expect the gifts to cease until the return of Jesus.

Likewise, the writer to the Hebrews says that God testified to his message by 'signs, wonders and various miracles, and gifts of the Holy Spirit' (Heb 2:4). Nowhere in the Bible is the supernatural display of the power of the Holy Spirit confined to any particular period of history. On the contrary, such signs, wonders and miracles are part of the kingdom which was inaugurated by Jesus Christ and continues to this day. Hence we should expect today to see the supernatural display of the power of the Holy Spirit as part of his kingdom activity and as an authentication of the good news. However, we do not draw ultimate attention to the signs and wonders, but to the God of love who performs them.

Evangelism in the power of the Holy Spirit is both dynamic and effective

On the Day of Pentecost such was the power with which Peter preached that the people were 'cut to the heart' and 3,000 were converted (Acts 2:37-41). The remarkable events continued: 'Everyone was filled with awe, and many wonders and miraculous signs were done by the apostles.... And the Lord added to their number daily those who were being saved' (Acts 2:43-47).

Remarkable healings followed (eg Acts 3:1-10). People were astonished and came running to find out what had happened (3:11). Peter and John preached the gospel with great boldness: 'When they saw the courage of Peter and John and realised that they were unschooled, ordinary men, they were astonished and they took note

that these men had been with Jesus. But since they could
see the man who had been healed standing there with
them, there was nothing they could say' (Acts 4:13-14).
The authorities had no idea what to do because 'all the
people were praising God for what had happened. For
the man who was miraculously healed was over forty
years old' (Acts 4:21-22).

The dynamic effect on the crowds continued:

> The apostles performed many miraculous signs and wonders
> among the people. And all the believers used to meet
> together in Solomon's Colonnade. No-one else dared join
> them, even though they were highly regarded by the people.
> Nevertheless, more and more men and women believed in
> the Lord and were added to their number. As a result, people
> brought the sick into the streets and laid them on beds and
> mats so that at least Peter's shadow might fall on some of
> them as he passed by. Crowds gathered also from the towns
> around Jerusalem, bringing their sick and those tormented by
> evil spirits, and all of them were healed (Acts 5:12-16).

People continued to be converted. 'So the word of God
spread. The number of disciples in Jerusalem increased
rapidly, and a large number of priests became obedient
to the faith' (Acts 6:7). As we go on in the book of Acts
the same pattern continues. When Paul and Barnabas
went to Iconium, 'they spoke so effectively that a great
number of Jews and Gentiles believed' (Acts 14:1). They
spent a considerable time there 'speaking boldly for the
Lord, who confirmed the message of his grace by
enabling them to do miraculous signs and wonders'
(Acts 14:3). In Lystra a crippled man was healed (Acts
14:8). In Derbe 'they preached the good news in that city
and won a large number of disciples' (Acts 14:21).

Later on, Luke tells us what happened to twelve
Ephesian men: 'When Paul placed his hands on them,
the Holy Spirit came on them, and they spoke in tongues

and prophesied' (Acts 19:6). Further, in Ephesus, 'God did extraordinary miracles through Paul, so that even handkerchiefs and aprons that had touched him were taken to the sick, and their illnesses were cured and the evil spirits left them' (Acts 19:11-12).

Far from dwindling away through the period covered by the book of Acts, this spiritual dynamic continued. Even in the last chapter we read of Paul praying for Publius' father: 'His father was sick in bed, suffering from fever and dysentery. Paul went in to see him and, after prayer, placed his hands on him and healed him. When this had happened, the rest of the sick on the island came and were cured' (Acts 28:8-9). All the way through we see the dynamic effect of the coming of the kingdom of God accompanied by conversions, miraculous signs, healings, visions, tongues, prophecy, raising the dead and casting out evil spirits. The same God is at work today among us. Evangelism can still be dynamic and effective.

Effective evangelism requires the filling and refilling of the Spirit

Jesus told his disciples, 'You will receive power when the Holy Spirit comes on you; and you will be my witnesses in Jerusalem, and in all Judea and Samaria, and to the ends of the earth' (Acts 1:8). On the Day of Pentecost the promise of Jesus was fulfilled and 'all of them were filled with the Holy Spirit and began to speak in other tongues as the Spirit enabled them' (Acts 2:4).

However, it did not end there. Later on we read of Peter being 'filled with the Spirit' again (Acts 4:8). Still later the disciples (including Peter) were filled again (Acts 4:31). The filling of the Holy Spirit is not a one-off experience. Paul urges the Christians of Ephesus 'to be filled with the Spirit' (Eph 5:18) and the emphasis is on

continuing to be filled. Professor Wayne Grudem writes
the most useful chapter I know of on this subject in his
masterful *Systematic Theology*.[9]

As we look at the great evangelists of more recent
history we see how many speak of such experiences.
John Wesley (1703-1791), the founder of modern
Methodism, wrote of an occurrence on New Year's Day
1739:

> At about three in the morning, as we were continuing in
> prayer, the power of God came mightily upon us. Many
> cried out in complete joy. Others were knocked to the
> ground. As soon as we recovered a little from that awe and
> amazement at God's presence, we broke out in praise.

The result was that 'the Holy Spirit began to move
among us with amazing power when we met in his
name'. When anyone fell down under the preaching,
they were prayed for until they were 'filled with the
peace and joy of the Holy Spirit', which was frequently
'received in a moment'. Wesley's journal is full of such
accounts. One Quaker, who objected to such goings on,
'went down as thunderstruck' and rose to cry aloud:
'Now I know you are a prophet of the Lord.'

Wesley concluded: 'Similar experiences continued to
increase as I preached. It seemed prudent to preach and
write on the work of the Holy Spirit.'[10] He preached
regularly at Bristol's Newgate prison where the jailer,
Abel Dagge, had been converted under Whitefield in
1737.

> One Thursday Wesley preached on the text 'He that
> believeth hath everlasting life' and at the end he prayed 'If
> this is thy truth, do not delay to confirm it by signs
> following'. Immediately 'the power of God fell among us.
> One, and another, and another, sank to the earth ...
> dropping on all sides as thunderstruck'. One, Ann Davies,

cried out. He went across and prayed over her and she began to praise God in joy.[11]

For thirty-five years George Whitefield (1714-1770) was the outstanding itinerant preacher in Britain and America and he changed the conventions of preaching, opening the way for mass evangelism. He wrote in his journal: 'Was filled with the Holy Ghost. Oh, that all who deny the promise of the Father, might thus receive it themselves! Oh, that all were partakers of my joy!'[12]

Charles Grandison Finney (1792-1875) was one of history's greatest evangelists, considered by many to be the forerunner of modern evangelism. Finney's experience of the Holy Spirit occurred later on the same day as his conversion.

The Holy Spirit descended upon me in a manner that seemed to go through me, body and soul. I could feel the impression, like a wave of electricity, going through and through me. Indeed, it seemed to come in waves and waves of liquid love; for I could not express it in any other way. And yet it did not seem like water but rather the breath of God. I can recollect distinctly that it seemed to fan me, like immense wings: and it seemed to me, as these waves passed over me, that they literally moved my hair like a passing breeze. No words can express the wonderful love that was shed abroad in my heart. I wept aloud with joy and love; and I do not know but I should say, I literally bellowed out the unutterable gushings of my heart. These waves came over me, and over me, and over me, one after another, until I recollect I cried out, 'I shall die if these waves continue to pass over me.' I said, 'Lord, I cannot bear any more;' yet I had no fear of death.[13]

Perhaps the greatest evangelist of the nineteenth century was D.L. Moody (1837-1899). Early on in his ministry he was a successful superintendent of a Sunday school mission in Chicago. However, two old ladies in his congregation informed him after a service that they were praying for him because he lacked the power of the Spirit. Although he was annoyed at their suggestion, the more he pondered about it the more he knew they were right. He wrote later that 'there came a great hunger into my soul. I did not know what it was. I began to cry out as I never did before. I really felt that I did not want to live if I could not have this power for service.... I was crying all the time that God would fill me with His Holy Spirit.' About six months later, as he was walking down Wall Street in New York City, the Holy Spirit came upon him powerfully. He wrote later:

> Oh! What a day, I cannot describe it! I seldom refer to it, it is almost too sacred an experience to name ... I can only say God revealed Himself to me, and I had such an experience of His love that I had to ask Him to stay His hand.

John Pollock, his biographer, adds that Moody needed never thirst again. 'The dead, dry days were gone. "I was all the time tugging and carrying water. But now I have a river that carries me."'[14]

Moody's successor at his Bible Institute was the great American evangelist of the early nineteen hundreds, R.A. Torrey (1856-1928). In his book *The Baptism with the Holy Spirit* he wrote:

> It was a great turning point in my ministry when, after much thought and study and meditation, I became satisfied that the baptism with the Holy Spirit was an experience for today and for me, and set myself to obtain it. Such blessing came to me personally that I began giving Bible readings on the subject, and I have continued to do so with increasing frequency as the years have passed.... It has been the author's unspeakable privilege to pray with many ministers and Christian workers for this great blessing, and after to learn from them or from others of the new power that had

come into their service, none other than the power of the Holy Spirit.[15]

In his book *Why God Used D. L. Moody* Will H. Houghton wrote:

> Some of our readers may take exception to Dr Torrey's use of the term 'the baptism with the Holy Ghost.' Perhaps if Dr Torrey lived in our day and saw some of the wildfire in connection with that expression, he would use some other phrase. But let no one quibble about an experience as important as the filling of the Spirit. In this little book Dr Torrey quotes Mr Moody as saying, in a discussion on this very matter, 'Oh, why will they split hairs? Why don't they see that this is just the one thing that they themselves need? They are good teachers, they are wonderful teachers, and I am so glad to have them here, but why will they not see that the baptism of the Holy Ghost is just the one touch that they themselves need?'

I think that there can be little doubt that the greatest evangelist of our century has been Billy Graham (b. 1918). In his authorised biography John Pollock tells how Billy Graham visited Hildenborough Hall and heard Stephen Olford speak on the subject 'Be not drunk – but be filled with the Spirit'. Billy Graham asked to see Olford privately and Olford expounded the fullness of the Holy Spirit in the life of a believer. 'At the close of the second day they prayed, "like Jacob of old laying hold of God,"' recalls Olford, 'crying, "Lord, I will not let Thee go except Thou bless me", until we came to a place of rest and praising;' and Graham said, 'This is a turning-point in my life. This will revolutionise my ministry.'[16]

One of the keys to Alpha is having a team of Spirit-filled people using every gift they possess to lead others to Christ. Those who come to Christ on the course know that a radical change has occurred in their lives because they have been filled with the Holy Spirit. This experience of God gives them the stimulus and power to invite their friends to the next Alpha.

In the rest of this book I want to look at the practical outworking of this vision and intersperse it with stories of some of those whose lives have been changed by attending an Alpha course.

Testimony 1

NIGEL SKELSEY

2
Nigel Skelsey

Nigel Skelsey rose quickly to the position of picture editor of a national newspaper, but felt he had 'lost his soul in the process'. He joined an Alpha course at Holy Trinity Brompton and subsequently wrote a letter about the effect it had had on his life. With his permission, the letter is reproduced here.

Dear Nicky,

I was going to start this letter by saying, 'Just a short note to tell you what the Alpha weekend meant to me', but I'm afraid it's turned into a long note. Please bear with me, but it's something I feel I need to get down on paper.

In 1979 my father died of stomach cancer and it was at that time that my Christian faith went on the back burner, and for the last fifteen years I haven't known why. It wasn't, as one might suppose, the question of suffering and a loving God. That wasn't a problem for me. I have subsequently found out it was far more deep-rooted than a moral dilemma.

For most of my life I have felt I've been a huge disappointment both to God and my parents. When I left school I spent three years at theological college training to be a church minister with a genuine desire to be an evangelist, but I failed academically, ending up with the double burden of not only being looked upon by my parents as a failure but also, I felt, by God as well.

I decided to pursue a career in photography, which was a hobby of my father's, with the hope of winning my parents' approval, and I joined a publishing company as a tea boy on a newly-launched photographic magazine. I had been there six months when my father got ill and eventually died. Just two weeks after his death the staff, on what was an ailing magazine, were sacked or left of their own volition. The tea boy was the only one left and was promptly made editor by default. It was success of sorts and something of which my father would have been incredibly proud. But he wasn't there to see it and I was devastated.

For the next fifteen years there followed a faithless and obsessive pursuit of success for its own sake. Every time I achieved something I would knock it on the head and start again from scratch. I was like a child with building bricks. I would build a tower and shout, 'Look, Dad!' before knocking it down and building another one to impress him with.

My career was like a roller-coaster. The ailing magazine, more by luck than judgement, given my inexperience, was turned round and within two years was the biggest selling monthly photographic magazine in the country. At the height of its success, and after only two years in the job, I left to join another magazine which was in a poor state. Within two years circulation was surging to the point of overtaking the first magazine. Once more success came quickly, but it wasn't enough and after another two years I put an end to that and decided to launch my own photographic magazine which, within no time at all, became renowned around the world, picking up publishing awards along the way.

Another two years had gone by and I still wasn't satisfied, so in 1987 I decided that I wanted to be picture editor of a national newspaper. I had no experience in that particular industry and to all bar the totally demented it did not enter the realms of possibility. Since I was fast joining the ranks of the totally demented I didn't see the problem and within three years, at the grand old age of thirty-seven, I became the picture editor of the *Sunday Telegraph*.

Just before Christmas 1993 I turned forty and, probably like many on reaching that age, decided to reflect on what I had achieved and possibly where the next challenge lay. Forgetting the spiritual side, which was non-existent anyway, I was very satisfied. I had everything I had ever wanted in life: a fulfilling, well-paid job, a beautiful wife, two great sons, and, at one point I'm embarrassed to say, a Porsche 911. But at what cost?

I discovered that my nickname at *The Telegraph* was 'The Beast'. Despite the affectionate undertones that many nicknames have, it told me something about myself that I didn't like. I also overheard someone else say that I was not truly happy unless I was at war with someone. They were right. In fact, if conflict didn't happen to come my way then I created it. Life had become a great battlefield.

Jesus said, 'Love your neighbour as yourself,' but my trouble was that deep down I hated myself and I hated my neighbour as myself. My motto was: 'Forget revenge, get your retaliation in first!' I was like some ageing prize fighter who doesn't know when to give up. Every single day of the last fifteen years has been a brawl, only, unlike a boxing match, the bell never came at the end of each round. Worst of all I looked in the bathroom mirror one morning and saw reflected back someone I just didn't know any more. Over the next few days the words of Jesus kept coming back to me, 'What good will it be for a man if he gains the whole world, yet forfeits his soul?', and I realised that I had done just that. In my own little world I literally had everything I ever wanted but I had lost my soul in the process.

Then on New Year's Day a friend whom I hadn't seen for years came round to dinner. What struck me was that he wasn't the person I used to know. Even though a Christian, my old friend was the most dreadful pessimist whose character I despised; the new version sitting in front of me was full of vigour, optimism and genuine happiness. And he started to tell me about the great work that the Holy Spirit had done in his life. He went on to describe how he had felt a failure all his life and how his father had been hugely disappointed in him and, without warning, I burst into inconsolable floods of tears at the dinner table: something The Beast was not prone to doing!

He was describing what was locked away deep in my subconscious and, although I didn't realise it, had been dominating my life all these years. Unrattled, he stood up and prayed over me and I felt the most extraordinary tingling sensation flooding through me, flushing out all the deep-rooted unhappiness that had slowly festered beneath the surface over the years.

I had experienced something I didn't understand, but which had a profound effect on me. I woke up the next morning like a man obsessed with a new ambition. I sensed God loved me and that I wasn't a write-off in his eyes. I was still heavily chained at the bottom of a deep dark prison, only someone had banged a hole in the wall and a chink of light was spilling in, giving me a taste of the freedom that was there if only I could grasp hold of it.

In the summer I had been on holiday in Switzerland and had read an article in a magazine I found about the Alpha course at Holy Trinity Brompton. The one thing that had stuck in my mind was how the work of the Holy Spirit was described as of paramount importance. I knew in my heart I had to have his power in my life at any cost so I found out where the church was, enrolled on the course and focused on the weekend. I felt like a dying man waiting for a life-saving operation. Never mind the weeks of pre-med, I just had to get into the operating theatre.

The weekend I had been waiting for, like a child waiting for Christmas, finally arrived … and I didn't want to go! I didn't realise what a spiritual battle I was about to experience. I lay in bed at the conference centre on the Friday night and went through an onslaught the like of which I have never experienced before and I hope I never do again. Voices screamed in my head to get out, go home, I was making a fool of myself, God wouldn't do anything for me, I was beyond hope, I was a failure and so on. I tried to pray but I couldn't. I just lay there for what seemed like hours and got the biggest mauling of my life.

I woke up in the morning shattered. I looked at the order of play, saw that the third session (which I had identified as the main one) was at 4.30 pm and simply hung on like a marathon runner weaving his way up the final straight with nothing but the finishing tape as the focus of his attention.

I'll never forget that final session. I felt as though I was being torn in two. Halfway through I just couldn't stand it any more. The prize was so near but we were getting there so slowly! I literally wanted to scream out, 'Do it now! Do it now! I can't hold out any longer.' I'm not exaggerating when I say I was in agony. Then God came, and oh, the relief.

Do you know, for the first time in my life I feel normal. It seems a strange thing to say but it keeps hitting me just how normal I feel! I also feel loved. I am accepted for who I am and I feel free. Terribly clichéd, isn't it? But I feel so free!

Yesterday I read some words of Paul in Philippians which express so deeply how I now feel about my 'achievements' of the last fifteen years: 'But whatever was to my profit I now consider loss for the sake of Christ. What is more, I consider everything a loss compared to the surpassing greatness of knowing Christ Jesus my Lord, for whose sake I have lost all things. I consider them rubbish, that I may gain Christ and be found in him.... But one thing I do: Forgetting what is behind and straining towards what is ahead, I press on towards the goal to win the prize for which God has called me heavenwards in Christ Jesus' (Phil 3:7-9, 13).

I don't know what the future holds or where and how God will lead me; at the moment I'm just enjoying a honeymoon period! Which brings me to the point of this letter. Thank you for helping to bring to completion what was started on New Year's Day.

Regards,

Nigel.

3
Practicalities

When explaining what Alpha is I find it helpful to use a mnemonic which sums up some of the ingredients on Alpha and goes like this:

Anyone can come. Anyone interested in finding out more about the Christian faith can be invited on this ten-week introduction designed for non-churchgoers and new Christians. It can also be used as a refresher course for mature Christians.

Learning and laughter. The course is based on a series of fifteen talks which tackle the key questions at the heart of the Christian faith. (These can be given by a leader or there are tapes or videos available if the group is small.) We believe it is possible to learn about the Christian faith and to enjoy the experience. Laughter and fun are a key part of the course, breaking down barriers and enabling everyone to relax together.

Pasta. Eating together gives people the chance to get to know each other and to develop Christian friendships. It is important that the course is held in a welcoming environment.

Helping one another. The small groups encourage everyone to participate and help each other along the way, as they discuss the talks, study the Bible and pray for each other. For the helpers themselves the course provides an opportunity to help bring others to faith. People often come back and help on the next course or bring their friends along to see what it's all about.

Ask anything. Alpha is a place where no question is regarded as too simple or too hostile. People are given a chance to raise their questions and discuss relevant topics in small groups after the talk.

Alpha courses vary in size. We have had experience of both small and large courses – we started as a very small group – and the principles in this chapter apply to all.

A typical evening

6.15 pm   Leaders and helpers meet to pray
7.00 pm   Supper is served
7.40 pm   Welcome
7.50 pm   Songs of worship
8.00 pm   Talk
8.50 pm   Coffee
9.00 pm   Small groups
9.45 pm   Finish

The meeting of the leaders and helpers at the beginning of the evening for prayer and organisation is of great importance.

At 7.00 pm supper is served. When Alpha was small (around twelve) each person on the course took it in turns to cook supper (starting with the leaders and helpers). As it grew we reached a point where we had over ten small groups. Each small group then took it in turns to cook supper. (We do not make a charge for the Alpha course, although a small contribution is requested for the meal each evening and for the food and accommodation during the weekend.) This system was totally restructured when we reached over 200 and had to employ a caterer and ask for slightly more for the supper to cover the costs.

Eating together is an essential part of the course, as it gives people the chance to get to know others in a relaxed way. Friendships grow over the course, especially within the small group, in an extraordinary way.

At 7.40 pm I welcome everyone and advertise books

and tapes. I also use this time to talk about the weekend
and the supper party at the end of the course. Then I
usually tell some kind of joke. I have found that humour

is an important part of the course and these jokes are
appreciated out of all proportion to their merit. It is
important for outsiders to see that we have a sense of
humour and that laughter and faith in Jesus Christ are
not incompatible.

At 7.50 pm we have a short period of singing. I explain
carefully what we are going to do. I often quote what the
apostle Paul says in his letter to the Ephesians, 'Speak to
one another with psalms, hymns and spiritual songs.
Sing and make music in your heart to the Lord' (Eph
5:19). I explain that we are going to sing a mixture of
psalms (usually set to modern tunes), hymns and
spiritual songs. We have a mixture of old and new. We
always start the first night with a well-known hymn for
the benefit of those who might find that more familiar.
As the course goes on we tend towards more modern
songs, changing gradually from singing about God to
singing directly to him, and we increase the length of
time we spend in worship from about five minutes on
the first night to about fifteen to twenty minutes towards

the end of the course. We try not to move too quickly at the beginning and I explain that what matters is that we 'sing and make music in our hearts'. Some may not be ready to participate and it is fine for them simply to listen until they are ready to join in.

The worship leader must sound confident, even if he or she is not. We have found that it is better that the worship leader gives no introduction to the songs. He or she is there to lead worship rather than to give what easily becomes another talk. Unless worship can be led and music played competently it is probably better not done at all. Some Alpha courses run without any singing. It is not an essential part of the course. The very small courses who listen to the tapes or watch the video would not normally have any singing.

I have found that although many find the singing the most difficult part of the course to begin with, and some are even hostile towards it, by the end they often find it is the part they value most. For many, such singing is their first experience of communicating with God. It also helps people to make the step from Alpha to the church, where the worship of God is central.

After the singing we have the talk. This may be given by the leader or a helper. On smaller courses it is probably better to have a variety of speakers. On larger ones it is necessary to have someone who is used to speaking to more sizeable gatherings. This inevitably limits the number of speakers available.

(In the next few paragraphs, when referring to a chapter in the book *Questions of Life*,[17] which is based on the Alpha talks, I will use the abbreviation QL followed by the chapter number.)

The first week the talk is on 'Who is Jesus?' (QL 2). In weeks two to six we cover the material in Chapters 3-7. At this point we often have a weekend away. If we do, then the talk on week seven is 'How can I resist evil?'

(QL 11). If the weekend away is at any other time 'How can I resist evil?' would follow after it. This is because I have found that the talk about spiritual warfare only becomes really relevant after people have experienced the power of the Holy Spirit.

On week eight we look at 'Why and how should we tell others?' (QL 12). On this week I start to talk about the supper party at the end of the course. The following week we look at the subject of healing (QL 13). There are no small groups that night as we stay together for ministry (see Chapter 11 in this book).

On the final night we look at the subject of the church (QL 14). The main aim of this talk is to start integrating those who have been on Alpha into the life of the church. We explain how the home group system in the church works and encourage them to join such a group. Often the whole small group on Alpha will join the same home group.

At the end of the talk on a normal evening we would go into small groups (see Chapter 7 in this book) and aim to finish at 9.45 pm.

At the end of the course we give people questionnaires (see Appendix D). The responses on these help us to see how the course needs to be improved next time.

The weekend

The weekend away is a crucial part of the course. This is the time which is devoted to teaching on the work of the Holy Spirit in the individual lives of those on the course. The material covered is in Chapters 8, 9, 10 and 15 of *Questions of Life*. It is possible to cover this material in a single day. Sometimes we have a Saturday locally for those who cannot make one of the weekends. However, there are enormous advantages to the weekend away.

We have found that friendships are formed on a

weekend much more easily than on a single day. As
people travel together, have meals together, go for walks,
enjoy the evening entertainments and receive Holy
Communion together on Sunday morning, there is a
cementing of friendships which have begun to form in
the early weeks.

It is in this relaxed environment that people unwind
and some of the barriers begin to come down. I have
found many make as much progress spiritually
during the weekend away as in the rest of the course
put together.

I know that it is hard to find a venue but it is usually
possible if plans are made far enough ahead. If members
of the congregation cannot afford to go away, then the
weekend could take place in a local venue. However, in
most congregations it is possible for those who can
afford a little more to pay for those who cannot afford to
pay anything at all or only a part.

The timetable for our weekend is as follows:

Friday

6.30 pm onwards	Arrive
8.00-10.00 pm	Supper
9.45 pm	Worship and a short introduction to the weekend
	This can include a brief talk based on John 15 or perhaps a testimony

Saturday

8.45 am	Breakfast
9.30 am	Worship
	Talk 1 – Who is the Holy Spirit?
10.45 am	Coffee
11.15 am	Talk 2 – What does the Holy Spirit do?
12.00 noon	Small group discussion. Often we look at 1 Corinthians 12:1-11 and

	the subject of spiritual gifts
1.00 pm	Lunch
Free afternoon	Activities can be organised, eg, sports, walks etc.
4.00 pm	Optional tea
5.00 pm	Worship
	Talk 3 – How can I be filled with the Holy Spirit?
7.00 pm	Supper
9.00 pm	Revue. A variety of sketches and songs without anything distasteful, religious, or nasty. Participation is voluntary!

Sunday

9.00 am	Breakfast
9.45 am	Small group discussion. An opportunity for each guest to talk about what they have seen and heard so far
10.30 am	Worship
	Talk 4 – How can I make the most of the rest of my life?
	Holy Communion
1.00 pm	Lunch
Free afternoon	Hopefully everybody meets again at the evening service at church

Preparation

First, the dates need to be fixed. The course takes eleven weeks (including the party at the end). Alpha at Holy Trinity Brompton takes place on Wednesday evenings (although there is also a daytime Alpha – see Appendix C). It is of utmost importance, in order to maintain the momentum, to run *at least* three courses a year. We used to run four a year, but due to the size we have had to cut down to three. We have found that the best times are during the Autumn term (October to December), Spring term (January to April) and Summer term (May to July).

Secondly, a venue needs to be found. The ideal venue is a home. For many years the Alpha course at Holy Trinity was run in a home. We had considerable hesitations about moving from a home because such an environment is unthreatening for those who do not go to church. We only did so eventually because of the increasing size of the course. When the course outgrows the home, a venue needs to be found with a welcoming atmosphere.

Thirdly, the course needs to be advertised so that those outside the church and those on its fringes can be attracted. Once the congregation have confidence in the course they will invite their friends. As an Anglican church, we also encourage adults who are preparing for baptism, parents wanting to have their children baptised, and also confirmation candidates to do the course. I even encourage couples who are intending to get married in the church to do it as part of their marriage preparation. Some have said to me that it was the best possible marriage preparation as it transformed not only their relationship with God but also their relationship with each other. We would also advertise the course at services which attract those on the fringe, such as the services at Christmas and Easter.

In addition I find it a help to advertise the course on the two Sundays prior to the beginning. On these two Sundays we give out brochures with the service sheets. On the first of the two Sundays in both of the services, in the notices, I explain what Alpha is (using the mnemonic at the start of this chapter). Then I interview someone who has just done the course. I choose someone with whom people will find it easy to identify and about whom they cannot say, 'I can see why he or she needs Christianity, but it's not for me.'

The best people to interview are those who are not very keen. This is because if they agree, then they are only speaking for the benefit of others and not for themselves. I usually ask people about ten minutes beforehand. If they are asked any further in advance they begin to write things down and the interview loses its freshness and power. In those ten minutes I often ask them the same questions I will ask them for real later. This gives them a chance to practise and me a chance to pick up on anything interesting. I also give them lots of reassurance that all will be well! In an interview I normally ask them to say something about what they felt about Christianity before the course, what happened to them and the changes Jesus has made in their lives. I ask them to avoid glittering generalisations. Rather they should be specific and give concrete examples of the changes that have occurred.

On the second of the two 'Alpha Sundays' before the course begins we often have guest services. These services are designed to make it easy for people to bring their friends who would not normally go to church. The service is kept short and the talk is aimed specifically at dealing with the questions often raised by those who are not Christians. At the end of the talk we suggest that those who would like to investigate Christianity further come along to Alpha on Wednesday. We do not ask them to identify themselves as we find that most of those who are not used to going to church wish to remain anonymous. I suggest they come along to the first night of Alpha. I tell them that if they don't want to come back no one's going to ring them up or send them junk mail. This takes the pressure off them. Most who come to the first night continue to come of their own accord.

The other place we advertise Alpha is at the celebration suppers, but I will say more about that towards the end of this chapter.

Selecting a team

When starting an Alpha course the first task is to choose a leadership team. If the course is going to be a large one (thirty plus) the team will need to include an administrator and possibly a worship leader.

Approximately one third of the course members should be leaders and helpers. Each small group is made up of around twelve people of whom three or four are leaders and helpers. These need to be selected very carefully. The leaders must be those who appear to have the beginnings of a gift of evangelism. They do not necessarily need to be Christians of many years' standing, but one indication of this gift is that they are 'good with people'. This is the test I often use when someone suggests someone, say John, as a leader: 'Suppose you had a non-churchgoing friend for whom you had been praying for several years; would you be totally confident about putting them in John's group?' If the answer is 'No' they are probably not suitable to be a leader of a small group on Alpha. If the answer is 'Yes' then they are likely to be a good leader.

In every group we also have one or two helpers, usually one man and one woman. They might be a couple or two single people. We do, however, try not to have a boyfriend and girlfriend leading or helping with a group, as complications can arise if the relationship breaks up halfway through the course. The ideal is to have one couple and two single people on the leadership team of each group. The helpers should pass the same test as the leaders but they may be relatively new Christians. Indeed, occasionally they may not even be Christians at all. Many of our helpers are those who have just finished the previous course. Some ask to come back and do the course again. In many cases I would ask them to come back as helpers. I strongly discourage anyone from simply repeating the course. I do not want people to get stuck doing Alpha over and over again. They need to move on in their journey of faith. One of the ways of moving on is to come back and help others. People who have recently done the course are often specially sensitive to the fears and doubts of members of their group. They can empathise with them, saying, 'I felt that,' or, 'I found that difficult.' This removes the 'us' and 'them' barrier.

As well as those who request to come back, I ask the leaders of the previous course to recommend those from their small group who they think would be good at helping. I myself look out for those I think would make good helpers and ask them to come back and help. Many of them are new Christians and many have lots of friends who are not Christians. Quite a high percentage of the next course will be friends of those who are helping. This is one of the ways in which the course grows.

If the course is large it is helpful to have what we call a task force. These are people who perform practical tasks such as catering, washing up and moving chairs. They are vital to the smooth running of the course. They do not take part in the small groups as they are fully occupied with the practical tasks. We have a remarkable group on the task force. They are people who either do not want to be in a small group or would not be suitable for a small group but have 'the gift of helps' (1 Cor 12:28). They are like the group chosen in the Acts of the Apostles to 'wait on tables' (Acts 6: 2). They are men and women who are full of the Spirit and willing to serve in any capacity. Their love and service are in themselves a powerful witness to the love of Christ to those who are on the course.

Training the team

It is vital that all the team (including those who have

been Christians for many years) are trained. Leaders, helpers and task force are invited to the training sessions. We run three evenings of training. Two are usually held on the two Wednesdays before the course begins. The first talk is on pastoral care (see Chapter 5). The second is on leading small groups (see Chapter 7). The third training session is usually held on a Monday evening, just before the first weekend away. This session is on the subject of ministry (see Chapter 11).

On the training evenings we meet at 7 pm for supper. It is important that the team should spend time together and get to know each other before the course begins. We don't assume that they already know each other very well. At 7.45 pm we begin with worship and prayer. All the way through we stress the importance of praying for the course. We then have the talk and an opportunity to ask questions either relating to the talk or about any other aspect of the course. At this point we cover some of the administrative details and prepare people for the jobs they will be asked to do on the first evening and thereafter. We aim to finish each training session at 9.45 pm.

The celebration supper

We begin talking about the supper party at the end of the course around week seven. On week eight (when the talk is on 'Why and how can I tell others?') we advertise it and give out the invitations. On week ten we try and work out the final numbers of those coming. When Alpha at Holy Trinity Brompton was small, each person would bring a certain amount of food. These days we use caterers, since we now have over a thousand people attending, and those on the course contribute as they are able, bearing in mind the number of guests they intend to bring.

On the actual evening of the celebration we invite

people to arrive for a drink at 7.15 pm (guests are asked on the invitation to bring a bottle of wine or soft drinks) and we have a sit-down dinner together. We do not say grace as we do not wish to embarrass guests. At around 9 pm I welcome everyone. We usually thank those people who have been involved in the organisation of the evening. I then invite one or two people who have taken part on the course to speak about what has happened in their lives, giving them the minimum of advance notice so that they do not have too long to worry about it. I do not allow them any notes as it always comes out best when they speak from their hearts about their own experience, and I always interview them so that they do not need to worry about forgetting what to say. After the interview I give a talk along the lines of 'Christianity: Boring, Untrue and Irrelevant?' (QL 1). If the party is at Christmas I give a similar talk but based around the theme, 'What is the point of Christmas?'

At the end of the talk I usually refer to Paul's experience in Athens where he found there was one of three reactions to what he had said about Jesus (see Acts 17: 32-34). 'Some of them sneered.' I point out that that was my own position for many years, so I am not judging them if they take the same position. Others said, 'We want to hear you again on this subject' (v 32). I suggest that those who feel like that come to the next Alpha course for which we have invitations and brochures available. Finally, 'A few … believed' (v 34). For the benefit of these, I ask everyone to bow their heads for a prayer and then I pray a prayer aloud along the lines of the one in the back of the booklet *Why Jesus?*[18] There are usually some, I discover afterwards, who pray the prayer that night.

I then encourage anyone interested to come, at least, to the first evening of the next Alpha course. I offer every single guest a copy of *Why Jesus?* I invite them to stay for

coffee, more food and chat. Most of them stay and talk
with the friends they came with and the evening finishes
around 11 pm. Many of those who come to the supper
wish to do an Alpha course as soon as possible. Hence it
is vital that there is one planned immediately thereafter.

The Alpha supper is one of the reasons why so many
people come on each Alpha course. We have found that
each Alpha supper has been bigger than the one before
and each Alpha course likewise has been bigger than the
one before. Therefore, it is good to make sure that in each
group people are organised to lay tables, serve and wash
up, or chaos may ensue.

After Alpha

In practice, the strong friendships often formed on
Alpha mean that the small groups want to stay together
afterwards. However, new Christians need to be
integrated into the life of the Christian community, and
the appropriate ways of doing this will vary. With
thousands of Alpha courses now running, there have
been many requests for more follow-up material suitable
for use in a house group setting.

In response to this, we are compiling a programme of
adult Christian education which now includes the
following: *Questions of Life* (ie Alpha), *A Life Worth Living*,
Searching Issues and *Challenging Lifestyle* (two terms).

These resources are described in more detail at the
back of this book, their broad aim being to give people
solid biblical roots for their new faith and lifestyle, and
to address problems and difficult issues in a clear and
simple way.

Sometimes people ask me whether Alpha is always a
success story. They want to know if every person who

comes on the course becomes a Christian, is filled with the Spirit, gets excited about Jesus, and brings hundreds of friends to the next course. Unfortunately the answer is, 'No, it's not always like that!' We surveyed a recent course which had around 400 guests and found that between 60 and 80 people had dropped out. When we analysed why, we found the following reasons.

First they stopped coming because of us. We did not run the course as well as we might have done. For this reason we have questionnaires at the end of the course so that we can constantly improve them and make them more user-friendly.

Secondly, people drop out for good reasons. For example, some people move to another part of the country. Increasingly, however, people are able to carry on the course where they move to. I know of one couple who started the course in London and finished it in Hong Kong! Another man did weeks 1-7 at HTB, week 8 in Boston, where he was on business, and then finished the course with us in London. This shows the advantage of the Alpha register.

Thirdly, people drop out for reasons connected with the parable of the sower (Mt 13:3-8, 18-23). Jesus said that some people's hearts are hard: they are simply not ready to hear and they often leave after the first evening. Sometimes they come back on the next course, or a year later. One person came back after four years and said to me, 'I have never forgotten what I heard the first night.'

Some drop out because of personal troubles in their lives, or through persecution or ridicule. Somebody may laugh at them and say, 'What are you doing going to church on a Wednesday?' Many of the people who come on the course lie about what they're doing on Wednesday nights. One man told me that a friend of his had come over from New Zealand and asked him out for a drink on a Wednesday night. As he was going to Alpha he gave a vague excuse: he was not prepared to admit what he was doing. So his friend said, 'Oh that's a pity,' and he looked through his diary.

'How about next Wednesday?'

He explained that he was busy, but had difficulty justifying why he was busy the next Wednesday and the next. Finally he admitted to being on a course.

'What course is that?' the friend asked.

'Oh,' he replied, 'I am learning French.'

Many are not prepared to admit that they are on a course about Christianity because they fear ridicule.

Jesus also outlines a third category of people for whom the cares of this world, the delight in riches and the desire for other things come in and choke the word. We've found that a relationship or success at work or some other distraction may take people away either during or even after the end of the course.

And that leaves the fourth category, which Jesus called the good soil. This bears fruit, thirtyfold, sixtyfold or even a hundredfold. The minimum is thirtyfold. I was very encouraged by the second group I ran. None of them were Christians but all of them came to Christ, were filled with the Spirit, and they are all now involved in the leadership of the church. I have kept in touch with all of them, except one. I had no idea what had happened to her, until we went and ran a conference in Nairobi. When we arrived there our host got us together in his house. I walked in and there was this girl called Nataya who I'm ashamed to say I didn't recognise. But as we walked into the room she started jumping up and down, a Masai way of showing excitement. She said that she had been praying for four years that Alpha would come to Kenya and she is now involved in running courses there. So all those people who came bore fruit: it was an amazing group. In the following group only one person stayed all the way through but she brought her husband

and several of her friends to the next course. The seed that falls on good soil bears fruit thirtyfold, sixtyfold, a hundredfold.

Testimony 2

MARTIN BENNETT

4
Martin Bennett

From the age of twelve, Martin Bennett was the victim of a man who gave him drink, abused him and forced him to keep everything secret. It went on for almost a decade. Here Martin tells the effect that had on his life and how God lifted the 'terrible burden of guilt' and one afternoon changed his life.

I was brought up a Catholic, but thought that God was something that you may come across when you're dead. I wasn't too sure. As time went on, my attitude changed and I became very anti-God, anti-Jesus and anti-religion.

When I was around twelve years old, I was abused by a teacher in my school. He was a Catholic teacher, a single man and a high-profile member of the local church. It all went on for a number of years.

He used to get me very drunk. The first time I remember drinking Scotch was when I was at his place and he used to do things to me when I was drunk, a lot of which I can't remember. I think that's partly me blocking it out. He was an alcoholic. I can't remember many times when I'd be with him when I wasn't drinking or drunk. He put me in a position where I couldn't get out, and made me imagine that everything I did was wrong but that it was supposed to be kept secret. If I told other people about it then that would be very bad indeed. He would tell me secrets, confiding in

me about other teachers, about other people in the
community. I was therefore forced into a situation where
I was emotionally attached to him when I didn't want
to be. My way around it was to switch off my
emotions completely.

I left that school when I was thirteen and went to
secondary school so I got away from him in the school
environment but in fact it got worse. As I got older, he'd
take things away from me that I would need. It would
start with things like my train pass. It might be money,
my passport or anything like that. He'd take them away
if I didn't contact him. So I would have to contact him
and then the whole cycle would start up again. I was
always covering my tracks – leading a double life in fact
– from very early on. He was perceived to be a fine,
upstanding member of the community. My parents did
not know what was going on. Half the time they knew I
was with him and that was acceptable to them because
they still thought we had an OK relationship. No one
knew what was going on, although I suspect my
brothers had an inkling but were scared to come near it.
I think they were frightened to think this could be
happening. And I would have denied it to the ends of
the earth.

I got to the stage in my early twenties when I still
hadn't completely broken free from it. I was still seeing
him off and on, but it wasn't with the same intensity. I
knew I had to try and get away. I travelled around the
world for two years or so, and he used to track me down
in Australia and things like that. As a result of all this –
and I do connect the two very strongly – I grew very
dependent on alcohol at an early age. I was drinking to
make life easier and to try and forget things because I
realised that if I drank enough, everything became a bit
of a blur. It blocked things out of my mind. This
continued for many years. I was drinking heavily from

about sixteen or seventeen. The whole business was a huge great lead weight and I assumed that I'd carry that around with me always.

After I came back from travelling, I got involved with drugs. When I was twenty I was hospitalised for quite long periods of time with attacks of acute pancreatitis, which can be an alcohol-related disease. When I had these attacks I was given high levels of pethidine, which is a very strong painkiller to which I became addicted. I was told not to drink but this also became part of my double life as everyone assumed I wasn't drinking and all the time I was. It was part of my life that went into the 'secret file'. Most of the time I would go to sleep quite drunk.

I started off drinking a small amount of Scotch or vodka every day, but ended up drinking an awful lot by the end. It was usually vodka because I had heard people say you can't smell vodka. But if you wake up the next morning still drunk it doesn't matter what you've been drinking. During my longest stay in hospital, at the Middlesex, they were giving me Heminevrin to help with the alcohol withdrawal, pethidine to help with the pain ... and I was drinking at the same time.

I had been going out with a girl called Catherine for a while and she realised something serious was going on. Eventually, it all came to a head, and thank God it did. I was twenty-six years old. I went to see various psychiatrists, psychologists, psychoanalysts, psycho-therapists. Some were OK; some were awful; some were useless. I was still very reluctant to let everything out, but it was obvious to everyone that I was an alcoholic, so I went to a detoxification centre for about three months down in Epsom.

When I was at the detox centre, the story of the schoolteacher and what he had done began to come out. I never wanted anyone to know about it. I didn't want to tell the police and I didn't want a big thing made of it. But when people said, 'What if he's doing it to someone else?', then I felt morally obliged to talk to the authorities. As far as I know he was never prosecuted. But he's not teaching any more and he can never teach again.

Then I went to a halfway house in Queenstown Road, Battersea, and that was good. I had stopped drinking and that was great. I was really making progress. Catherine stood by me throughout this time. She was my constant source of strength and support. Without her I don't know what would have happened. Our relationship was obviously an awful lot better because I had stopped drinking. But there were still a lot of things that weren't right. I had the odd relapse with alcohol and these were very difficult times for Catherine. We got married in July 1992 and at that stage I hadn't been in hospital for a few years. We were married in a church, as both our parents were Catholic and it just seemed the right thing to do. (I didn't really get married in church for any other reason.) At the time, I was working for a film company as a camera technician.

Then in November Catherine heard from her cousin about the Alpha Course at Holy Trinity Brompton. She thought she'd go along and see what it was like and so tagged on to the last half of the current course and she thought it was really great. I thought she was getting involved in some sort of cult and was a little bit concerned. However, she's a very sensible girl and so I thought that it couldn't be anything particularly bad. None the less it was certainly nothing that *I* wanted to get involved in. I would argue with Catherine a lot. My inbred dislike for any religion came out and it got to the stage where she wouldn't mention it to me any more because she knew I would want to argue.

Then Catherine got her cousin, Madeleine, with her

husband, Con, her brother Michael, her sister Clare, her sister Anna and Anna's boyfriend, Tim, all to do the next Alpha course which started in January 1993. So they'd troop off every Wednesday night, and then went off to the weekend away and came back on an incredible high. Of course it was just emotionalism to me. I was still very, very cynical about the whole thing. Catherine would go off to church on Sundays and for a time she would ask me if I would come to church. I always used to refuse, but then after a while I stopped to think about it. There was such a change in Catherine.

She seemed to have an inner peace. I thought, 'I'm married to her. I really ought to check this out because if I don't, I won't know if I've missed anything.' So I came along to Holy Trinity Brompton on a Sunday evening and the first time I came I thought, 'Gosh, what a bunch of wallies.' But the one thing that stuck in my mind was the worship. Ric Thorpe was the worship leader then and I saw in him someone very much like myself. He just seemed a normal person. Every time he got up on the stage he looked like he was still laughing from a joke that someone had told him before he got up. I thought, 'I want to know what that joke is all about. I want to know why he looks so happy. And why are all these people so happy?'

So I went along the next week on the strength of that, and Catherine prayed (I didn't know this until later on) that I'd be touched by the Holy Spirit during the service. And I was. I didn't realise what it was at the time but I just felt this incredible peace come over me. During the worship, I broke down in tears. I was sitting down and everyone else was standing up and I was crying, crying my eyes out and I couldn't work out what was going on. I was in floods of tears. I couldn't stop it. I put it down to emotionalism and getting a bit caught up in the event. I was still quite anti-Holy Trinity Brompton but I decided I would do the Alpha course to give it a chance.

I went along to the first Alpha evening and agreed with most of the things I heard about the historical evidence of the existence of Jesus and the Bible and I thought, 'Yes, that's pretty good. I don't believe it, but that's pretty good.' But, I thought, 'If I'm going to get any benefit from this, I ought to discuss it with someone and try to clear away some of the cobwebs.' So I decided to ring Nicky Gumbel the next day. I said to myself, 'I'm going to try ringing him twice and if I don't get to speak to him then that's it. I will have tried.' I rang the first time and he was out and I thought, 'This is looking good.' I rang the second time and he was there and said, 'Yes, come along and see me today at 5.30 pm.'

So it was that on a summer's evening, 6th May 1993, at 5.30, I went along to Nicky's place. We went into his back garden and he said to me, 'Tell me a bit about yourself.' And I told him my life story. What was strange was I told him everything in one go which I'd never really done before. I'd been to see psychiatrists and psychologists and bits and bobs had come out but I just sat there in that back garden in Clapham and it all came out. It all seemed to be coming out in surprisingly frank detail which had never really happened before, and after about half an hour, he said to me, 'Well, do you feel like praying?' And I said 'No, not really,' because I didn't. But he said, 'OK. You don't have to pray but I'm going to pray.' So I said, 'Fine. Carry on.' He prayed out loud for me and as he was praying I decided, 'OK. I'll close my eyes.'

And this incredible peace came down on me. It was an overwhelming presence of goodness. Everything seemed so safe. He just carried on praying and after a while he said, 'I feel a very strong presence of God. Do you feel it?' I said, 'Yes, I do as well.' I couldn't believe it! And he said, 'Well, look, I've got this prayer written down in *Why Jesus?* Do you think you're up to praying it now?' And I said, 'Yes, I think I am.' Everything was pointing in that direction for me. It was a prayer turning away from everything I knew that I'd done wrong and asking God to come into my life.

In it is the line that says, 'I forgive all those who have wronged me' – or words to that effect – and Nicky said to me that he wanted me to include the name of the guy who had abused me when I was younger and to say that I forgave him. This was quite a thing to me. The whole idea of forgiving him was totally beyond me, totally beyond my comprehension. But I said that I forgave this man. I said it three times, and each time my burden got lighter, so that by the third time I felt I was rising up into the trees. I felt an incredible release of this weight that had been dragging me down. It was lifted from me. I knew that I'd forgiven this person and that God had forgiven me. I had carried around all the guilt for a long, long time. It was quite incredible!

I opened my eyes again and there were tears pouring down my face, and it was the same with Nicky. He said something to the effect that he never fails to be surprised and amazed by the power of God. And I said, 'Well, I agree!' What had happened to me was something that was amazing – so powerful, so relevant and so unique. There was nothing like that when I went to see any of the psychiatrists or whatever. There was no comparison. It was total cleansing. Total forgiveness is way, way beyond anything you'll ever find in a book; any sort of Jungianism or Freudianism or anything like that. They just pale into insignificance compared to forgiving, being forgiven and starting a relationship with Jesus.

We had a friend coming round for supper that evening and I wanted to tell Catherine what had happened. I saw our friend trying to park outside and so I ran out of the door shouting back to Catherine: 'I've just been round to see Nicky Gumbel and I've given my life to Christ.' And she thought, 'What!' But once she understood what I was saying she was delighted. It was lovely.

Incidentally, the fellow who came to dinner that night who wasn't a churchgoer, has just done the Alpha course and is helping on the current Alpha course.

I went and told my mother the next day and I've never seen her happier. It was incredible. She had been praying for me for a long time. I drove down the A3 to my parents' house with tears streaming down my face listening to tapes of praise and worship music. I needed windscreen wipers on my eyes really. There were lots of tears of joy, happiness … Oh, unbelievable happiness. It was great!

My father, who is a more traditional Catholic, also recognised that something quite significant had happened to me. I wrote to my in-laws, who had also been praying, and they were very happy. The following Sunday in church Sandy Millar invited anyone who wanted to receive the Holy Spirit up to the front. I went and, as I was prayed for, I felt the Holy Spirit rushing into me. He filled me up. I had been feeling a little bit vulnerable, but once I really felt I'd got the Holy Spirit on board I thought, 'I can cope with anything.' I had that power and that reassurance.

I carried on with the Alpha course and everything began making sense to me then. All my pseudo-intellectual arguments disappeared. All the cynicism went. It was incredible! I was happy! It has made such a difference to Catherine and our relationship. We have been to a few weddings since ours and the marriage vows spring out of me now. They mean so much more. We try to pray every day and have a prayer group with the people I met on my first Alpha course. I pray for the man who abused me on occasions. I've realised that he's obviously a very lonely, very mixed-up, very sad person. He's not a problem for me any more.

It has all been such an answer to prayer. Catherine was praying her head off during that time when she was going to Alpha without me. She had a prayer diary and we've been looking back at it. It's got things like 'Prayed that Martin does go to church.' That's got a tick by it. 'Prayed that Martin does the Alpha course.' That's got two ticks by it. 'Prayed that Martin becomes a Christian.' That's got a great huge tick by it, and lots of other ticks with a little smiley face!

5
Pastoral Care

The first words of Jesus to Peter (in Mark's Gospel) were: 'Come, follow me … and I will make you fishers of men' (Mk 1:17). In his last conversation with Peter (in John's Gospel) Jesus repeated, 'Follow me!' (Jn 21:19) and urged Peter to feed and take care of the sheep and the lambs. The first priority is our relationship with Jesus. The second is our relationship with others.

In this last recorded conversation with Jesus on earth, Peter tells Jesus three times that he loves him. Each time Jesus' response is to tell Peter to look after other people. If we love Jesus, we will make this a high priority in our lives. Indeed it is part of following Jesus' example. He had compassion on people and once compared his longing to care for them and look after them to a hen with her chicks (Lk 13:34).

King David was a man who had experience of pastoral care as a shepherd tending sheep and also in the sense of being a shepherd of God's people. The psalmist says that 'David shepherded them with integrity of heart; with skilful hands he led them' (Ps 78:72). Pastoral care involves our *hearts* and our *hands*. We must have an integrity of heart: our love for people and our friendship with them must be genuine. There must be no false pretence. This love needs to be combined with 'skilful hands'. There are skills which we can learn. Obviously in a short chapter we cannot look at all the skills of pastoral care but I want to mention some of the general principles involved in this area.

The apostle Paul wrote: 'We proclaim him, admonishing and teaching everyone with all wisdom, so that we may present everyone perfect in Christ. To this end I labour, struggling with all his energy, which so powerfully works in me' (Col 1:28-29).

Aims

Paul's aim was to 'present everyone perfect in Christ' (v 28). Some versions translate the word for perfect as 'mature'. Perfection is not something we can reach in this life, but it is possible to become mature. Three vital points emerge from this verse.

First, Paul's concern is for *everyone*. A good pastor will not want to lose any of his sheep. The aim on Alpha is that every single person should be looked after, which is why each group has two main leaders and two helpers. The idea is that one of the leaders or helpers should take responsibility for each of the members in the group. It is a flexible and very relaxed system but the clear aim is that everyone on the course should receive care and prayer.

This system of one-to-one care is perhaps the most crucial aspect of Alpha. For myself, I owe so much to the man who helped me on an individual basis, early on in my Christian life. He sacrificed his time to answer my questions, explain the Christian faith to me and to give me advice, guidance and friendship. It was always fun to be with him: indeed, it was the highlight of my week as he helped me to lay the foundations of my Christian life.

Care like this is much more likely to meet people's needs. Preaching and teaching are inevitably like throwing a bucket of water over empty bottles, whereas one-to-one pastoral care is like filling each bottle individually from the tap. Not only is it the most effective method, it is also a form of Christian service in which everyone can take part as it does not require great speaking or leadership gifts.

Juan Carlos Ortiz tells the story of meeting an old lady in his native Argentina, who introduced him to a young girl who was one of her great-grandchildren. She went on to tell him that she had six children and thirty-six grandchildren. Her family was impressive in number and among her grandchildren were many well-educated and professional people. Ortiz asked her, 'How did you manage to produce such a large, well-fed, well-dressed, well-educated, extended family?' She replied, 'I didn't. I just took care of the six and each of them took care of their six.'[19]

Preachers can overestimate the amount of truth that is assimilated between the pulpit and the pew. Bill Hybels and Don Cousins, leaders of the 19,000-strong Willow Creek Community church near Chicago, have spoken about their experiences of coming to realise that sermons in and of themselves do not prepare people to live effective Christian lives. Hybels states that every major strategic step or decision he has made was inspired and encouraged by someone three feet from him and not in a crowd of a thousand people. 'Truth applied across a table' has been a key to his own personal growth.

Secondly, our aim in this one-to-one pastoral care is *spiritual maturity*. Of course, this cannot happen overnight or even during a ten-week course. The leaders' and helpers' aim is to assist people through the early stages and then integrate them into a group within the life of the church, where they can grow and mature further.

The groups on Alpha are arranged, right from the start, with this express aim. That is why, ideally, the team in each small group should come from the same home group and at least one of the leaders or helpers should

go with the group back to that home group and help
introduce and integrate the new members.

Thirdly, Paul's aim is maturity *in Christ*. We do not
want to attach people to ourselves but to Christ. Good
parents encourage independence in their children. They
begin by feeding their children but teach them, as soon
as possible, to feed themselves. We need to beware of
any unhealthy dependence on us and help people to
become dependent on Christ.

Our aim is that every person who comes to Alpha
should come to spiritual maturity in Christ. In practice,
of course, a number of people drop out. Our surveys
have shown that about 20% do not complete the course.
Half of these people drop out for good reasons, eg
moving away.

Some drop out the first night and we often do not
know the reason why. Others leave because of the
teaching – for example, on sex before marriage. Others
find friends laugh at them for going to church and they
are put off for that reason. For others still it is 'the
worries of this life, the deceitfulness of wealth and the
desires for other things' (Mk 4:19).

As in the parable of the sower those for whom the seed
falls on good soil, 'hear the word, accept it, and produce
a crop – thirty, sixty or even a hundred times what was
sown' (Mk 4:20). That is why we find that however many
people drop out, the next course is almost invariably
larger than the one before.

Method

Paul's method was to proclaim Christ. He wrote, 'We
proclaim *him*, admonishing and teaching everyone with
all wisdom' (Col 1:28). Jesus Christ is the key to spiritual
maturity. We grow in maturity as our knowledge of him
and intimacy with him grow.

Many of those who come on Alpha are not yet Christians. The aim is to lead them to Christ. They may give their lives to Christ during one of the main sessions or they may do it on their own. But every leader and helper should know how to lead someone into a relationship with Christ. *Why Jesus?* is the booklet we use on Alpha as a resource in this area. I use it myself when explaining the Christian faith to those who are not Christians and then I encourage them to pray the prayer in the back of the booklet. Sometimes they will want to pray it on their own, but more often they would prefer to pray it out loud with someone (see Martin Bennett's story in Chapter 4).

Once people have come to Christ, it is vital to encourage them to grow in that relationship. Bible reading and prayer are the keys to this. We need to help them with reading the Bible and advise them as to how they might pray on their own. We can give practical advice about which translation of the Bible might be appropriate to buy and guide them towards some suitable Bible reading notes. And it is good to explain that Bible reading is not an end in itself but a means of experiencing a relationship with Jesus Christ (Jn 5:39-40).

As well as the Bible, Christian books can be a great help. We encourage people to read a balanced diet of doctrinal, biographical and devotional books. Some are not great readers and prefer to listen to tapes of the Alpha talks and other subjects. We find many people enjoy listening to them in the car or when working around the home and this reinforces their faith.

In order to become mature in Christ, people need to grow in their relationships within the body of Christ. The small group is the ideal place to start developing such friendships. As weekly meetings proceed, friendships grow quite naturally. We can encourage the process by acting as a catalyst for discussion in the early stages, when people don't know each other well. Later, if they start coming to church, it can help if group members arrange to meet and sit together. If any of them live near each other, giving lifts encourages both the person who is giving the lift and the person who is receiving it, to come regularly.

Attitude

In helping people on Alpha to grow into maturity in Christ, we have found three principles to be of great importance:

Encouragement

In his early Christian life, Paul was much encouraged by Barnabas. He in turn became a great encourager (Acts 16:40; 20:1-2). He also wrote urging Christians to 'encourage one another and build each other up' (1 Thess 5:11). In the world there is so much negative criticism, leading all too often to insecurity and timidity. People shrivel up emotionally in an atmosphere of criticism and they thrive in an atmosphere of love and encouragement. We need to express warmth and responsiveness to those who are searching or are new Christians.

Listening

James writes, 'Everyone should be quick to listen, slow to speak…' (Jas 1:19). It is the task of the team on Alpha to draw out the guests and listen to them. We should take a genuine interest in them and encourage them to speak about themselves. If guests have ideas which are contrary to the Christian faith, we should not be quick to correct them. First, we need to listen, to try to understand where the other person is coming from and to show respect for people even if we disagree totally with their ideas. If they reach a point where they are interested and intrigued enough to ask us what we think, they will pay far more attention to what we have to say.

Peacemaking

Jesus said, 'Blessed are the peacemakers' (Mt 5:9). It is important for the team on Alpha to be gracious and courteous and to avoid getting involved in arguments.

On the whole, people will not be convinced if they get involved in an argument, especially if it is in front of others in the group. They tend to dig in their heels, which makes it harder for them to give up their position later if they wish to do so. It is easy to win an argument and lose a person. If there is an argument brewing, the leader should try to reconcile differences and relieve tension, diplomatically exploring reasons for the differences. Usually there will be an element of truth in both points of view and the leader can say, 'Isn't it a bit of both? Fred is right in saying … and George is right in saying....' Then both Fred and George feel affirmed and the argument is over. Obviously, truth is what matters but the truth needs to be spoken in love and we need to be careful that 'speaking the truth' is not an excuse for a personality clash, an expression of anger, or a wrong exertion of authority.

Commitment

Paul says, 'To this end I labour, struggling with all his energy, which so powerfully works in me' (Col 1:29). In Paul's pastoral care there was a balance between God's grace and his own responsibility. Our pastoral care should express the same balance. There is an element of 'toiling' and 'striving' involved in all effective Christian ministry.

Being on the team on Alpha involves a great deal of hard work. It requires a high level of commitment. Guests on Alpha are unlikely to reach a higher level of commitment than the leaders and helpers in their group. If the team does not attend regularly, those on Alpha are unlikely to do so. I ask leaders and helpers to rule out of their diaries all the evenings of the training course, as well as the ten Wednesdays of the course, the supper at the end and the weekend. Of course, occasions will arise when they are unable to attend, because they are abroad or required to work, or ill. But I ask them to give it the same priority they would give to their job.

This commitment is necessary because there are times when it will be a real effort to get there and talk to people sometimes until quite late at night. It requires an effort to talk to new people, rather than talking to friends. I ask people to pray and prepare beforehand so that when they are there they can concentrate all their efforts on the guests. This kind of effort makes for a very long evening.

Most important of all, helping on Alpha involves a

commitment to pray. We ask the team to come to the prayer meeting at 6.15 pm every Wednesday, if they can possibly get away from work by then. We also ask them to commit themselves to praying regularly for every aspect of Alpha: the worship, talks, ministry and administration, as well as praying daily, if they can, for the individual members of their group.

The other side of our responsibility is God's grace. We do not 'labour' and 'struggle' on our own. We do it 'with all his energy, which so powerfully works' in us (Col 1: 29). We need his help and his power for every task. When the disciples chose people to wait on tables they chose those who were 'full of the Spirit and wisdom' (Acts 6: 3).

I encourage all the team to receive from the Lord, both at the prayer meeting beforehand and during the main session, as they enter into the worship and listen to the talk. Even if they have heard the talk several times before they can pray that God will show them something new and relevant to their lives. All the time I encourage them to pray for God to fill them with his Spirit and empower them with all the gifts they need: evangelism, teaching, pastoring and prophecy (the ability to hear what God is saying in a specific situation and pass it on to others).

It is this individual one-to-one pastoral care which is one of the most exciting aspects of Alpha. Members of the team often tell me thrilling stories about what has happened to an individual during the course. Not only has that individual's life been changed but it has brought great blessing to the member of the team who befriended him or her. There is no greater joy than to lead someone to Christ and watch them begin to grow in the faith.

The nineteenth-century evangelist R. A. Torrey, writing on the subject of pastoral care, said he believed that when the membership of any local church exercised its responsibility and privilege in this matter, and each and every member of church acted it out in the power of the Holy Spirit, 'a great revival will be close at hand for the community in which that local church is located. [It] is a work that wins but little applause from men, but it accomplishes great things for God.'[20]

Testimony 3

MARY STEPHENSON

6
Mary Stephenson

Mary Stephenson's mother prayed all her life that her daughter might come to faith in Jesus Christ. She watched as Mary became a drug addict, a thief and eventually an inmate of Holloway Prison – but she never stopped praying. She died in 1987. Here Mary describes how her mother's prayers were finally answered.

When I was six weeks old, I was adopted from the Catholic Children's Adoption Society into a good home. My adopted father was a diplomat and my mother was American. My mother was a devout Catholic and one of the things I truly believe is that it is through her prayers that I'm here today. I know that she prayed for me daily. I was raised in South America and when I was about ten I was sent to a convent boarding school in England. It was probably then that I started to get quite independent. It's not like being at day school where you can go home to Mum and tell her that you're upset about something. At boarding school I tended to sort out my problems myself. Sometimes I wouldn't see Mum and Dad for about four months.

I did my 'A' levels when I was seventeen. One of them was in theology, but I didn't read the New Testament, so I failed it. There seem to have been so many times when God has been in my life but I've ignored him completely

93

because I had no understanding. Nobody explained God to me.

I was off like a shot when I finished school. I moved up to London straight away and got involved with what I thought was a great crowd. I went to all the parties and took something called 'smack' which somebody gave to me saying, 'Snort this. It's really fab.' So I snorted it up my nose and thought it was such a wonderful feeling. I remember telling a girlfriend of mine, 'You've got to try this. It's so good,' and she said, 'Mary! Smack is heroin.' I said, 'Don't be so daft.' Of course if somebody had handed me a syringe with a needle on the end and said, 'Try this,' I would have said, 'On your bike,' because I always thought that heroin, syringes, junkies and Piccadilly Circus went together. But I snorted this apparently quite harmless powder and it was such a nice feeling. I didn't understand what all the fuss was about.

However it all soon led to 'chasing the dragon' and then mainlining. I spent the next six or seven years leading a life of deceit, dishonesty, lying and whoring … complete abuse. My friends were doing it and I wanted to be involved. To start off with, I used to buy it from them, but as time went on I got to meet the dealers. I really did dive in, but I thought I was all right because I always had a job of some description. I was doing secretarial work at the time. I used to say: 'Well, all my other friends who are junkies are unemployed so I can't be that bad because I'm in work.' I still had to have a fix to get up in the morning and one at lunch time and one in the evenings. But I went to work and I didn't actually realise what sort of state I was in.

I think my brother, who was a medical student at the time, began to notice but I convinced myself that I was leading a normal life. Mum and Dad were abroad, so they didn't really know too much about it. I didn't go home because I never had any money. Occasionally they paid for me to come home and then I used to get quite sick because I was withdrawing. I remember my mother thinking I had rheumatic fever because I was aching and shivering all over. Every time that happened I used to tell myself that I was never going to touch the stuff again. Then, as soon as I got off the plane when I got back to London, I 'scored' straight away.

I became very dishonest and was stealing cheques and things. Inevitably I got caught and at my first court case my dad really put his career on the line because he stood up in court for me. Unfortunately, the press got hold of it because, although I was nobody, my father was an ambassador in a country at the time. It really broke my parents' hearts and, although it wasn't their fault at all, they blamed themselves. I used to say, 'I'll be all right, Mum. I'll get my act together now.' Then as soon as they went off I'd go back to using.

I ended up in Holloway Prison because I got arrested for stealing. Dealers would acquire stolen cheque books and cheque cards and then they would say, 'You go out and buy this,' if it was a woman's cheque book and card. So I would pretend to be that person and buy whatever items the dealers wanted – or, more often than not, go into banks and cash the cheque, and get the cash for them – and they would give me drugs in exchange.

What goes on in prison is frightening. I have never been so terrified in my entire life. I couldn't believe what was happening. It's a very frightening and vicious circle and I am very glad that I was only in there for a short spell – about six to eight weeks.

I got out on the condition that I went to a clinic for a year on probation. My parents took me up there and Mum said to the director, 'Where's the nearest Catholic priest or church because I want to contact them so that they know Mary's here?' The director said to Mum: 'Look, lady, she's here to get off heroin. Religion? Forget it.' I remember saying to Mum: 'When are you going to learn? If there was a God don't you think he would have answered your prayers by now?' She prayed constantly for me.

My parents went back to Canada, where they were living at the time, and I spent a year in this clinic. That was in 1983. At the clinic we were completely humiliated. You began to realise the despair and anguish that you caused other people, but they had a very strange way of doing things. One time I tried to leave and as a result I was dressed in blue overalls and nobody in the clinic spoke to me. There were about sixty people there. My place at the meal table was set upside down and I had to do things like clean the swimming pool with a tea cup and toothbrush. I couldn't understand how they thought that was going to get you off drugs: it seemed it was just to humiliate you.

Unfortunately it all took its toll on my mum. She had had cancer years before. With all the stress and trauma, it came back in a big way and I know my family felt that I wasn't making things any easier. As soon as I came out of the clinic I 'scored' again with heroin. It was because my mind was not healed: I had been in that clinic through force, and until you yourself decide that you want to do something it just doesn't work. Eventually, though, I did get myself back on my feet and I got good jobs and travelled quite a lot. I got the most fantastic job working in Vancouver. My mum was dying and it meant that I could go and live there with them as my father was then working in Canada. I had got the job off my own bat as well. I was beginning to feel quite good about myself.

I was with my mother when she died in 1987. She was really at peace when she went. She had an incredible faith. When she died one of the things she said to me was that I would never be happy without faith. She begged me to go to church, the Catholic church, but I thought she was off her rocker. Back in England I went on to get good jobs but something was still not quite right. Although I had great relationships with men, there was something missing. My oldest friend Daphne Stewart-Clark had 'got religion' about three or four years before that and she was always telling me to come to church and I would say, 'Daphne...forget it!' I could see that it had made a really, really huge difference to Daphne, which was great, but I said, 'It is not for me.'

Some time later, I phoned Daphne at nine o'clock one morning before I went to work. I had been out the night before with a load of people and had got absolutely drunk. It was awful because I suddenly found the old feeling of oblivion coming back. I realised that I wasn't happy and I phoned up in tears and Daphne came straight round. She said, 'Come on, Mary. Let's pray.' So we did and I was in tears, and at that stage I would have gone for anything. She then said, 'Why don't you do this Alpha course?'

I went along to the church she suggested and hated it. So I told Daphne where she could put her Alpha course and she said, bless her, 'Well look, Mary, I'm going to be helping on a course at another church in April or May. Why don't you do it and then I'll be there?' So I said: 'Well....' And she said: 'Oh please, please give it a try.' That was the Alpha course at Holy Trinity in April or May of 1993.

I went and when everybody started singing I got very emotional. I found a real warmth and sincerity among the people that I hadn't seen before. They really cared. As I listened to the talks, it all really began to fall into place. Mark and Tamsin Carter, my group leaders, are now two of my closest friends. In the first group, Mark said, 'What would you like to pray for? Let's all pray for something and we'll see what happens during the course.' I was quite selfish and I thought, 'Well, all right. I need some real black and white signs here.' I said I wanted to pray for more gallery sales (I was working in a sculpture gallery) because things were absolutely dead. He said: 'All right, that's fine. Anything else?' And I said – I was being a bit flippant – 'Pray that I come back next week maybe.'

The following week I sold £85,000 worth of sculpture which I thought was a coincidence, but I went back because I felt that I had to go back and tell them.

I went back each week to Alpha, and soon it was time for the weekend away on the subject of the Holy Spirit. I didn't know whether I actually wanted to spend the weekend with a bunch of Christians. As it turned out, it was a very, very powerful weekend for me. Minutes into the first talk I was in floods of tears, and started shaking and sobbing. It was a very powerful feeling, but it was really safe. I can't compare it to anything I'd ever experienced before. I am so used to myself being dishonest that I would expect other people to be the same but it was wonderful and there was no doubt that God started working in my life.

On the Sunday morning James Odgers, who was leading the weekend, asked the Holy Spirit to come, and said: 'All those of you who want to ask Jesus Christ into your lives can say this prayer,' and he said a short prayer. I said it and I *really* said it. I asked God into my life and I asked him to sort me out. That really did happen. He came into my life but I still felt unworthy. It wasn't until a Sunday service later on that I actually felt that I had been forgiven. People saw me in tears and it didn't matter because I knew I was safe to do it in front of those people. I am completely cleansed and God has given me the most fantastic sign of his love.

I recently moved to a flat in North Kensington and soon afterwards I was on my way home when I saw a woman who had dropped her shopping. I helped her pick it up and as I looked up I saw a sign which said 'Catholic Children's Adoption Society'. It is right at the end of my road. I called my father and said, 'Dad, did you get me from the Catholic Children's Adoption Society in St Charles' Square?' He said, 'Yes, that's right.' After that, I went round and round on my moped looking at it and I thought, 'God really has wiped my slate clean. He's brought me back to start my life again from where I started it.' I felt God saying: 'Thirty-something years ago you started your life here. You went off down the wrong road and now I'm giving it back to you.' He has given it back to me and I've given my life back to him now. It's so true when the Bible says how God 'restores the years the locust has eaten'.

There were some people I hurt where I might never be able to make amends: one of those is my mum … I'm sure she's doing somersaults up there now. For once I am so content. I had never cried before, but at church I have cried a lot. The point is that there's always somebody there. Even if I'm at home alone and I'm crying, I know I'm not alone any more because God is there. That is a real comfort. I remember thinking the other night how I always used to have my fix next to my bedside table and I'd have a fix before I went to bed at night and then get it ready to have first thing in the morning. Now I've replaced that with my Bible. And I'm more passionate about the Bible than I ever was about my heroin. Indeed, my passion for heroin has been replaced by a far greater passion for Jesus Christ.

7
Leading Small Groups

John, a TV executive in his thirties, came with his wife, Tania, to an Alpha supper at the end of a course. Tania decided she wanted to do the next course, but John agreed to come along only reluctantly. He played little part in the discussion groups, apart from the occasional, rather negative, remark. On the weekend away he walked out of one of the sessions and told his wife they were leaving. She had become a Christian during the weekend and so was very disappointed. Nevertheless, she agreed to go with him. He told her on the way home that he was going to give up going to Alpha. I had not been involved in the weekend but Tania told me on Sunday of John's decision. So on the following Wednesday I was amazed to see him walk through the door. Later in the evening, when we were in small groups, we went around the group, each person reporting on their experience of the weekend. When it came to John, he told us what had happened. Naturally, I asked him why he had come back. He replied simply, looking at the group, 'I missed you lot.'

In John's case it was the small group which kept him coming to Alpha. He later gave his life to Jesus Christ and he and his wife are now firmly involved in the church. This incident shows us the vital importance of the small group.

The overall purpose of the small group, along with the course as a whole, is to help to bring people into a relationship with Jesus Christ. Jesus himself said that where two or three are gathered in his name he is there also (Mt 18:20). We have found that a group of about twelve (comprising two leaders, two helpers and approximately eight guests) is the ideal size. I do not think it is a coincidence that Jesus chose a group of twelve (Mk 3:13-19).

The six aims of the small group

1. *Discussion*

The groups meet to discuss the talk and issues arising out of the talk. It is vital to give people the opportunity to respond to what they have heard and to ask questions. This is especially the case if the group is made up predominantly of those who are not yet Christians. Usually such groups are not ready to study the Bible. When we first ran Alpha courses, the groups always studied the Bible from the first week. I soon realised that this was leading to considerable frustration. When the questionnaires came back at the end of the course there were comments such as, 'I only really enjoyed our group when we were allowed to spend the whole time discussing the talk.' Another wrote, 'I would have liked more time discussing the talk and more freedom to diverge from the set Bible study.'

The practical details are very important. The chairs need to be arranged so that everyone is comfortable and can see one another. Light and ventilation need to be good. Everyone should have access to a modern translation of the Bible. A good leader aims to keep the discussion to the set time. We aim to start at 9.00 pm and finish at 9.45 pm. I discourage leaders from going on as a whole group beyond this time, even if they are involved in a rip-roaring discussion. It is always possible to say, 'Let's continue this next week,' which will encourage people to return to continue the debate. If the groups go on too long, people may be put off from coming back, fearing another late night.

Some groups are ruined by one of two things. First, ineffective leadership, where the leader is not properly prepared or allows one person in the group to do all the talking. Or secondly, by an over-dominant leader who does all the talking instead of giving those on the course the freedom to speak and to say what is on their minds. The leader needs to be flexible enough to allow the group to change the subject, but confident enough gently to cut short 'red herrings' that are frustrating the majority.

It is important to ask simple questions. If you feel that the group is not ready for Bible study but discussion is not flowing very easily, possible questions to start discussion are listed in Appendix I of the training manual. Two basic questions to ask are 'What do you think?' and 'What do you feel?'

Leaders need to be prepared to help bring out answers to the issues raised in the group. I have found that some questions come up time and time again. The book *Searching Issues*[21] looks at the seven issues most often raised on Alpha. I encourage the leaders and helpers to be familiar with this material as well as reading around each of the subjects in it.

A good leader will always be an encourager. At the most basic level this means smiling at people and being and looking interested in what each person has to say. Even if someone says something that is not correct, a good leader will respond with a phrase like 'How interesting', or 'I have never heard that before', or 'It might mean that...', and will then bring in the rest of the group to try to reach the right conclusion.

2. *To model Bible study*

The second aim of the small group is to learn to study the Bible together and to grow in knowledge. As mentioned already, the leader should encourage the group members to do most of the talking and must resist the temptation to give a sermon.

Even if a Bible study is planned, it is important to give an opportunity to ask questions arising from the talk and to deal with these first. Otherwise, members of the group may feel frustrated that the real questions on their hearts and minds are not being answered.

If the group is ready for Bible study, the leader needs to prepare the passage carefully. He or she should read the passage in different versions and make sure they understand it. They should try and spot any difficult verses and look up the explanation in a commentary (in order to avoid wasting time in the groups).

In the group setting, explain where the passage comes in the Bible and give the page number, so that no one is embarrassed by their lack of knowledge. Sometimes it may be appropriate for each person to read a verse (for example, if you are looking at one of the Psalms); this gets everyone involved. For some passages (eg the prodigal son) it is better for the whole passage to be read by one good reader. Reading aloud can be a harrowing experience for some and they must be able to decline easily.

Then it is helpful to give a short introduction. For example, when studying the story of the prodigal son, one might begin by saying, 'Obviously, the father represents God and the son represents us. Let us see what lessons we can draw from the passage.' The introduction must be very short, perhaps one sentence, giving the main theme of the passage. It is a good moment to explain any obvious difficulties or ambiguous words. Leaders should be particularly careful to avoid using

Christian jargon which excludes the non-Christian and the new Christian.

Next, the leader has to get everyone talking. It is a good idea to work out the questions carefully in advance, and they should be kept short and simple. Questions that are either too vague (eg 'What is the difference between verses 7 and 17?'), too easy (eg 'Who died for us?'), or too difficult will not help to start discussion. Good questions to ask are open-ended ones that cannot be answered 'Yes' or 'No' and which provoke discussion of the key verses of the passage. The three basic questions to ask about any passage are 'What does it say?', 'What does it mean?' and 'How does it apply to our lives?'

The aim is to bring everyone into the discussion. Contributions from the quieter members of the group should be especially welcomed. If one person has done a lot of talking, it is good to ask, 'What do other people think?' Leaders should aim to learn as well as teach, and should not force their own ideas on the group. Even if we are asked directly for our own view, it is better, if possible, at first to deflect the question. Nor should we answer our own questions: it is better to re-phrase them.

Leaders should try not to repeat other people's comments unless they need clarifying for the rest of the group. If we are asked questions that we cannot answer it is fatal to bluff. We need to admit we do not know all the answers. Such an admission is often a good thing, and we can always tackle the question afterwards, or say that we will make a note of it and bring the answer next week. Better still, someone in the group might like to look up the answer. This helps the learning process, both for guests and for leaders. It is important we should not give the impression that there are easy answers to complicated questions or that we are great experts.

The most important thing is to make the study

practical, so that everyone can see how they should apply the principles, and how God can use the passage to change their lives. There is no need to study for too long – 45 minutes is plenty.

3. *To learn to pray together*

If the leader wishes to open in prayer, it must be done sensitively. The leader may pray, or better still, ask a member of the group to do so. However, it needs to be done very carefully. They need to be asked beforehand and it needs to be made clear to the rest of the group that this is the case. Otherwise, people will be afraid that next time they themselves may be asked to open in prayer. (I know of one or two people who stopped coming because they thought they might have to pray aloud.)

To avoid embarrassment, the leader could suggest a simple prayer (eg 'Will you ask God to give us wisdom to understand this passage?'), or, having asked someone beforehand, say to the group, 'I have asked X to open in prayer.'

Later on in the course, it may be appropriate to end with prayer. As most people find praying out loud quite daunting in the initial stages, it is important to talk about these difficulties and then model a very simple prayer, like 'Father… (short sentence) … for Jesus' sake. Amen.' This will encourage others that they could do something similar. Long eloquent prayers may be impressive, but they discourage others from praying. If we provide a simple model I have found that virtually everyone in the group prays, sometimes even those who are not yet Christians.

For those who do take the step and pray their first, faltering prayer, it can be a momentous occasion, giving new confidence to their relationship with God. It is deeply moving to hear someone's first public prayer. It is usually completely uncluttered by jargon and obviously comes straight from the heart. It is good to make clear to people that we all benefit when they muster the courage to pray aloud, however briefly and simply.

4. *To develop lasting relationships within the body of Christ*

It has often been said, 'People come to church for many reasons, but they stay there for only one: that they make friends.' We have found that extraordinarily close friendships are made during the course of the ten weeks. Four years ago I had a small group of twelve people, none of whom were Christians at the start of the course, but by the end they had all come to faith in Christ. All are now in positions of Christian leadership and remain very close. Immediately after the course, one of them said that before it had begun he had felt his 'friends register' was full and was amazed to find that he had made so many lasting relationships.

The leaders and helpers need to get to know each person in the group well. It is important to learn their names on the first night. Sometimes we play a name game to make this easier. Each evening the group sits together for supper and the leaders and helpers act as hosts and facilitate the conversations. Sometimes the group will go to a pub at the end of the evening, if people are comfortable with that. Sometimes they will meet up during the week, either on a one-to-one basis or all going out together as a group.

5. *To learn to minister to one another*

One small group I was involved in recently started out full of questions, some of which were quite hostile. They all seemed so different that I began to wonder whether they would all get on together, let alone minister to one another in the power of the Holy Spirit. But by the end it was wonderful to see them all praying for each other, laying on hands and praying for healing.

6. *To train others to lead*

Alpha has grown at such a rate that we continually need more leaders. It has grown from one small group to thirty-five small groups on the current course. Initially, the leaders were experienced Christians, often of at least ten years' standing. Many of the helpers these days have become Christians on the previous Alpha course and even the leaders may have been Christians for as little as six months. This is not ideal, but it is a good problem to have: presumably the early church was faced with a similar situation. When 3,000 were converted on the Day of Pentecost some of them must have needed to lead virtually straight away.

Paul tells Timothy to entrust the things he taught him 'to reliable men who will also be qualified to teach others' (2 Tim 2:2). It has been said that 'Delegation without training leads to disappointment', and we make sure that all leaders and helpers have done the three-session Alpha Training Course. The helpers can learn more about leadership from watching the leaders of their group 'in action', and it is hoped that the leaders' model may one day be useful to all the group members.

Testimony 4
LEE DUCKETT

8
Lee Duckett

When Mercury Telecommunications engineer Lee Duckett came to do a job at Holy Trinity Brompton one morning, he didn't realise that it was a visit which would change his life. After years of depression, he had asked God to reveal himself to him – and God did exactly that. Here Lee tells what happened.

I learned a little about Christianity at primary school. In assembly once a week they did an Old Testament or a New Testament story and they got the kids up to act it. But I just took it as something for kids. When I was about eighteen years old, I started reading science fantasy books and they influenced me quite a bit. I used to read a lot of books involving magic, gods, Arthurian history and also a lot of occult and New Age books. I considered myself an atheist although if I had to believe in some form of deity then I had more sympathy towards polytheism, as in the Norse or Greek gods, as I had read that they had been around longer.

I got involved with the occult after splitting up with my first girlfriend. We had been together four years, had got engaged, bought a flat and lived together for two years. After splitting I was heartbroken and we had to live in the same flat for six months as we had a negative equity mortgage. We saw each other on and off, in between her boyfriends, for another year and a half.

111

Then she asked if we could get back together. It lasted for about a month. Two weeks later she told me she was getting married to someone else.

I fell into a state of depression. I was trying to get over her and so started searching for things to do. I went to see a medium a couple of times, tried out a ouija board quite a few times and dabbled in magic. After a couple of frightening experiences I stopped the magic. All the time the depression was getting worse; I was starting to close in on myself and couldn't bear to be near people. I also had a lot of thoughts about suicide. I started a course of hypnotherapy and psychoanalysis which lasted about three months consisting of weekly sessions. This was extremely hard work but after the complete treatment I felt really good for about a month. Then the depression started coming back.

I had a couple of strange experiences when I tried praying to God. One was when I was in the bath and I started crying. For some reason I said a prayer, saying that I believed God was real and accepted him. I said, 'Well, if you're there let me know.'

A few weeks later, in the course of my work, I came to Holy Trinity Brompton. I turned up at about 9.30 am and for me it was just another job. I did the work I had to do – which was putting in a new Mercury Smart Box – and then started chatting to the girl at reception. I'd been thinking about buying a Bible and I thought I would just read it as a story. So I was talking to Perry [a staff member] at reception (and thought she was nice and everything, you know!) when I said, 'What's a good Bible to buy?'

She thought the NIV was probably a good one and then said, 'We do this course. Would you like to go on it?' At first I thought I wouldn't but we got chatting and she was really nice. I asked her if she went to church and she said, 'Yes, I go and I'm a Christian. My friends and I are

Christians and we have a lot of fun.' I couldn't understand what she meant at the time. I couldn't see how being a Christian was fun. She asked me again if I would like to do the course and I said, 'OK, then.'

Being an engineer, I've always been the type that reads the instructions on things first. I like to know what I'm doing. I like to do something in a set sequence. As Perry explained what the course was, I thought, 'At least you've got someone to teach you.' I like being taught things. I like finding things out, but why make it hard for yourself? I like things to be easy and I find it easier if someone's teaching me.

I was going to be away on holiday when the next course came up, so Perry booked me up for six months later in September. She then gave me a copy of the booklet *Why Jesus?* which I read later. I said the prayer at the end of it but nothing dramatic seemed to happen.

I found myself looking forward to the Alpha course and on the first night I arrived early and sat in my car in the car park for half an hour. I saw all these people going into the church and thought that there was some kind of function on. I thought, 'It's a bit late for a wedding. I wonder what's going on in there?' I was only expecting there to be about thirty people and so was duly shocked when I was taken into the church to see 300 people who looked normal. I couldn't believe it. It certainly wasn't what I expected. I thought they would be people who would speak strangely and wear pairs of glasses with little bandages on – anorak jobs and stamp collectors. I was really amazed by how young the people were and there were some really nice women!

My team leaders were Ashley and Sibs Meaney and I just couldn't believe how at peace Ashley seemed to be. I thought, 'He's got what I'm missing. He's got something I want.' When we started to sing I felt really uncomfortable as though I were back at primary school.

But I really enjoyed the talk and the group discussion afterwards and felt really good going home that night.

The next morning I woke up and started to have a wash and a shave. Then I looked in the mirror and this massive grin just came across my face and I started laughing. I was skipping around the house, laughing. I didn't know why. I just felt so happy. It was the first time I had smiled, *really* smiled, for about three years. I think with smiles you can tell by the eyes. With customers, I always put on this grin, but it wasn't a smile. My eyes were dead. But this time I smiled with my eyes too.

I bought an NIV Bible that Saturday and started at Matthew. I also started reading *Run Baby Run* by Nicky Cruz. Ashley invited me to church after the second Alpha evening and I felt really honoured to be invited. During that Sunday I spoke to Ashley about myself and my depression. That night the talk at the service was about depression. I stood up for ministry at the end and was prayed for by Ashley and his dad Baz. I felt their hands get really warm and I burst into tears and then felt a warm sensation rushing from my feet upwards, blowing the depression away.

During the following week I thought I was a Christian and tried telling some friends and family, but it was in an apologetic manner. Then over the next few weeks I started to become more at ease and was reading the Bible before going to sleep every night, reading Christian books and going to church on Sundays. One night, soon afterwards, I was in bed and after reading the Bible I started praying for the Holy Spirit to baptise me. I had been praying for about ten minutes and I felt as though there was a battle going on over me. All of a sudden I started thinking, 'Yea though I walk through the valley of the shadow of death I will fear no evil,' and I kept repeating this in my mind. I was really frightened. I then picked up my Bible and everywhere I opened it there were messages of the Lord's love and protection.

The next night I felt really uneasy in my bedroom and didn't sleep very well. The following day I phoned Ashley and told him about what happened. He said that he had been wondering when the Enemy would show up. He told me to get rid of the occult books and pictures in my room and to read Psalm 23 and Ephesians 6. The room did feel better after I had removed a picture and thrown some books away. That Wednesday the topic at Alpha was on evil. I had never felt so uncomfortable in church. I wanted to run. I felt nauseous and angry and wanted to leave immediately, but I did stay.

Then came the Alpha weekend, which was unbelievable. It felt as though we were developing real fellowship among the group and getting closer to the Spirit of God all the time. Nicky asked the Holy Spirit to come and fill us while we were all standing up. He said, 'He's working around the room,' and I heard and felt a blowing in my left ear. About two minutes later my knees started to buckle and I collapsed into my chair. I received the gift of tongues and at the end of the weekend I was full of joy and love for everyone.

We went to church that night and I was in the front row. I felt the presence of the Spirit all through the service. After the sermon we started to sing a song and I immediately felt God's presence and started to cry. Sandy [Millar, vicar of Holy Trinity] asked people to come forward for physical healing and I went forward for healing on my back. Sandy then asked the new Alpha people to help heal. A man called Ray came up to me and asked me what I wanted healing for. I said, 'My back,' and he asked if there was anything else, as my eyes were red from crying. I said 'No'. A husband and wife named Mike and Di from the Alpha task force came to help. I was taken to the side chapel and they started to pray for me. I felt the Spirit start from my feet and 'wash' through my body. I then felt the most unbelievably complete joy and began laughing uncontrollably. When it was all over I felt completely reborn. When I got home I prayed in tongues in the car for half an hour and slept like a log that night.

On the Monday evening I phoned around all my friends really excited and told them about the weekend and that I had become a Christian. This time I wasn't apologetic! My life has completely changed. I now look at this world through different eyes. I feel love for everyone and an inner peace that I never imagined could exist. Now when I meet people I want to tell them about Jesus and whenever I hear of people like the IRA, although I sometimes think, 'Scum,' 95% of the time I feel sorry for them and think, 'If only they knew Jesus like I am learning to know him.' I am also reading a lot of Christian books and I pray a lot in the car while driving.

My mum came to the Alpha supper. For Christmas she bought me a cross and chain which I didn't ask for. So I was really choked up about that because it shows she knows it means a lot to me. My mum and dad are just really pleased. All the family are. They take the mickey a bit. In fact they take the mickey a lot. But I keep inviting them to come. I feel the Spirit's presence almost every day. I obviously have many unanswered questions but just knowing God is enough.

9
Giving Talks

Before I was a Christian, I was dragged to a talk which was one of a series in a mission at Cambridge. I remember looking at the clock at the start, determined not to listen and watching it all the way through the talk, amazed at how long it went on and how bored I was. Others seemed to be enjoying it and laughing. But I had told myself that I would not listen to a word of it.

When speaking to Christians it is not unreasonable to assume an interest. We expect from the congregation a hunger to find out more about the Christian faith, to try to understand doctrine and study the Bible. With those who are not Christians we cannot make any such assumptions. Rather it is wise to assume they are asking, 'Why should I listen?' and are challenging us to say something of interest to them.

We need to respond to this challenge. In the opening words, we have to tell them why they should listen. Truth in itself is not necessarily of interest. Truth is not the same as relevance. If we start by saying, 'I want to expound the doctrine of justification by faith,' then they are likely to fall asleep. On the whole, people are not interested in theology or historical background until they see its relevance. We must arouse their interest right at the beginning: the first few seconds are vital.

They have got to think, 'This is interesting….' Like Jesus
we need to begin with a need, a hurt, or something else
of interest to the audience. Humour may be a way in,
providing it leads us on to what we want to say. On the
whole, people will listen to stories, whether they are
humorous or serious. These should then lead into a
subject of relevance to the hearers: work, stress,
loneliness, relationships, marriage, family life, suffering,
death, guilt, or fear.

In this chapter I want to look at the whole subject of
speaking to non-churchgoers (eg those on Alpha) and in
particular at giving an evangelistic talk (eg the Alpha
supper at the end of the course). I believe it is a skill
which many people could acquire. The major require-
ment is a strong desire to communicate the good news
about Jesus Christ. In preparing such a talk there are
seven vital questions we need to ask. We will look at
each of these in turn.

Is it biblical?

The Bishop of Wakefield, the Rt Revd Nigel McCulloch,
described a sermon, which he heard while he was on
holiday, as a 'disgrace'. 'The preacher spoke long, but

said little. There was no message. As I looked around at my fellow-worshippers I could see from the sleeping of the old and the fidgeting of the young that they, like me, were finding the sermon dull, uninspiring and irrelevant. What a lost opportunity. In fact, what a disgrace.' He did not reveal the content of the sermon, but he did observe that 'the congregation does not want third-rate personal comments on public affairs but real preaching that brings the Bible to life.... If St. Paul had been asked to advise the Church of England what to do in the Decade of Evangelism he would tell us what he told Timothy. In every pulpit, in every church, at every service "preach the word".'[22] This does not mean that talks to people who don't go to church must necessarily be biblical exposition. Rather they should be based on biblical truth and have verses of the Bible weaved into their fabric.

In giving an evangelistic talk at the Alpha supper at the end of the course there are certain ingredients that I always try to include. Paul said that when he went to Corinth he 'resolved to know nothing ... except Jesus Christ and him crucified' (1 Cor 2:2). I try to ensure that every such talk is centred on Jesus. First, I say something about who he is, that Christianity is a historical faith based on the life, death and resurrection of Jesus Christ, that the same Jesus is alive today and that it is possible for us to have a relationship with him. Secondly, I include something on 'him crucified'. I speak of what Jesus did on the cross when he died for us and how he made it possible for our sins to be forgiven and our guilt to be removed. Thirdly, I explain how someone can enter into a relationship with God, referring to repentance, faith, and receiving the Holy Spirit.

Is it good news?

In his first sermon, Jesus chose to preach on the text from

the prophet Isaiah, 'The Spirit of the Lord is on me, because he has anointed me to preach good news to the poor' (Lk 4:18). Jesus did not come to condemn the world but to save it. The gospel is good news in a world which is full of bad news. We should not simply make people feel guilty. We may need to talk about sin and guilt. But we do not want to leave people there. We are telling them about Jesus who frees us from sin, guilt and evil. That is good news.

When Philip spoke to the Ethiopian eunuch he 'told him the good news about Jesus' (Acts 8:35). I explain in the talk at the Alpha supper that Jesus Christ meets our deepest needs. I know that those listening who are not yet Christians will be struggling somewhere deep down with a lack of ultimate meaning and purpose in their lives; they will have no satisfactory answer to the inevitable fact of death or the universal problem of guilt. In all probability they will also be aware of a sense of 'cosmic loneliness', a sense of being in God's world without the God for and by whom they were made.

Aware of these needs I try to show how Jesus dealt with our guilt on the cross, how he defeated death by his resurrection, how he made possible a relationship with God which gives meaning and purpose to life, and how he gives us his Holy Spirit so that we need never experience that cosmic loneliness. Of course, the good news of the kingdom of God includes far more than this. But in a twenty-minute talk at an Alpha supper I stick to a few very basic parts of this good news. Whenever I have finished writing a talk I ask myself the question, 'Is this talk good news?'

Is it interesting?

We live in an age of TV and video games. People are not used to listening to long talks and it can be hard to retain

their attention. Undiluted theology will not grip most
people for very long. They prefer listening to stories and
hearing how the point of them fits in with their lives. As
a general rule, I find it helpful to follow the formula:
point, illustration, application. If a talk has three points it
will look something like this:

    Introduction
    (i) Point
         –   illustration
         –   application
    (ii) Point
         –   illustration
         –   application
    (iii)Point
         –   illustration
         –   application
    Conclusion

It is worth while collecting illustrations. They come
primarily from our own experience, but they can also
come from newspapers, radio, TV, films, plays, books
and magazines. Of course, many of the best illustrations
come from the Bible itself or from the natural world, and
we need to think out carefully the applications for our
listeners.

Is it persuasive?

Paul tried 'to persuade' people (2 Cor 5:11). We need to
work out what we are trying to achieve in a particular
talk. For instance, are we trying to lead people to Christ,
persuade them to start reading the Bible, or to pray? It is
worth writing down at the top of the talk what our aim
is. If we aim at nothing we are likely to hit nothing. If we
aim at too much our efforts are likely to be dissipated.

C. H. Spurgeon, the nineteenth-century preacher, said, 'One tenpenny nail driven home and clenched will be more useful than a score of tin-tacks loosely fixed, to be pulled out again in an hour.'[23]

Having established the aim we need to ensure that every point is focused in that direction, like a tent supported from three or four different angles. We need to use every argument to appeal to the minds, hearts and wills of the hearers.

There must be an appeal to the mind. We must give people reasons for doing what we are urging them to do. Over the Alpha course we try to teach all the basic elements of the gospel. At an evangelistic Alpha supper we try to teach the crucial elements of the good news.

If the talk were only appealing to the mind, it would be very dry. We need also to appeal to the heart. If, like me, you are British, you may find that hard. But people's emotions are involved as well. If it were purely an appeal to the emotions there would be a danger of emotionalism. Conversely, in appealing purely to the mind, we can stray into intellectualism.

Ultimately, if we are to persuade people to make a decision we need to appeal to their wills. In an evangelistic talk I try to drop a hint early on that there is a decision to be made, that there is no neutral ground, and there are no 'don't knows' in the kingdom of God. I let them know what the options are. They can refuse Christ or accept him or just put off the decision. All this must be done without any pressure. It is right to persuade but wrong to pressurise.

Is it personal?

Bishop Phillips Brooks defined preaching as 'the bringing of truth through personality'.[24] Of course, the message we want to get across is objectively true and much of what we say will be proclaiming that truth. However, it is a great help for the hearers if we can illustrate these truths from our own experience. We need to be honest and real, not pretending that we are perfect or that we never struggle in any areas of our lives. This does not mean that we have to make embarrassing public confessions, but it is a help to acknowledge our own difficulties and failures. Stories told against ourselves can be both amusing and encouraging at the same time, provided they are set in a context which builds faith and is not purely negative. For example, I often tell stories about my early attempts at evangelism and the ridiculous things I did. I do it partly as a joke against myself, but also to assure people that we all make mistakes.

It is wise to talk generally in terms of 'we' rather than 'you'. 'You' can be very threatening and it suggests that we are somehow putting ourselves above our hearers. 'We' is less threatening since it gives the impression that we are all in the same boat. 'I' is the least threatening since it does not intimate that the hearers have the same problems: if it is used too frequently, the talk will appear self-centred. Generally, however, I would suggest that 'you' and 'I' should be used sparingly. 'You' is often effective at the end of a talk: 'What do *you* make of the claims of Christ?' 'Will you decide today…?'

Is it understandable?

It is no use giving the greatest talk in the world if no one can understand it. It is often said that we should never overestimate an audience's knowledge and never underestimate their intelligence. Because knowledge is limited we need to avoid jargon (which is familiar only to the 'in' crowd) and technical terms such as 'justification', 'sanctification', 'holiness', 'atonement' or any other word which is not used in everyday speech. The only case for using such words is if we explain simply what we mean by them.

The other side of the coin is that because most people's intelligence is reasonably high, there is very little that they will not understand provided it is clearly explained. Many theological books and talks are incomprehensible to most people: reasonably enough, if they are technical books for experts. However, I know for myself that if what I am saying gets very complicated, it is usually because I myself do not fully understand it. Albert Einstein once said, 'You don't really understand something unless you can say it in a really simple way.'

Certainly the teaching of Jesus was basically very simple. His economy in the Lord's prayer, which comprises fifty-six words, is very favourable when compared to a recent EC regulation report on the sale of cabbages which totals 26,901 words!

Is it practical?

The Bible often exhorts us to be 'doers' rather than just 'hearers'. James writes, 'Do not merely listen to the word and so deceive yourselves. Do what it says' (Jas 1:22). Jesus himself said that what distinguished the wise man (who built his house upon a rock) from the foolish man (who built his house on sand) was that the wise man put into practice what he heard (Mt 7:24), whereas the foolish man did not.

If we are to help people put into practice what they hear, then we need to be very practical. We need to show them how they can do what we are talking about. In an evangelistic talk we should explain carefully what a person needs to do if they want to give their life to Christ. The vital elements in the New Testament response seem to be repentance, faith, and receiving the

Holy Spirit. I explain these using the words sorry, thank you and please.

I explain repentance in terms of asking forgiveness for the past and turning away from everything we know to be wrong (that is 'sorry'). I explain faith as putting our trust in what Jesus did for us on the cross ('thank you') and I explain receiving the Spirit in terms of asking him into our lives ('please'). Then I pray a prayer along the lines of the one in the booklet *Why Jesus?* and make it possible for them to pray that prayer in their hearts along with me.

Finally, it is good to remember that it is more important to prepare ourselves than to be prepared in the technique of giving talks. Billy Graham, speaking to 600 clergy in London in November 1979, said that if he had his ministry all over again he would make two changes. The audience looked rather startled. What could he mean? He said he would study three times as much as he had and he would give himself more to prayer. He quoted Dr Donald Gray Barnhouse who said, 'If I had only three years to serve the Lord, I would spend two of them studying and preparing.'

Testimony 5

DEREK AND FRANCIE LYGO

10
Derek and Francie Lygo

When Derek and Francie Lygo's three-month-old daughter Chloe was a victim of cot death two years ago, their world fell apart. Here Francie, who recently gave birth to their second daughter Freya, tells the story of what happened and how a new-found relationship with God has changed both their lives.

I've always been brought up in the Christian tradition. Derek was an atheist but we were married in church. It was love at first sight, and we were engaged within two weeks of meeting each other. We still love each other, probably even more than we loved each other then, if that's possible.

Ever since I was a child, I have always felt that there would be a time in my life when I would get to know God better. I didn't know when that would be but I knew it would be sometime. I don't think thoughts like that had ever even occurred to Derek. Life when we were married was going very well: he had a very good job in the City and we were on the crest of a wave. It wasn't always easy but we were very, very happy.

Then I became pregnant with Chloe which was the fulfilment of our dreams. We had wanted a baby as soon as we were married. We were thinking of moving into a bigger house and gearing up the mortgage. I did not have an easy pregnancy and I was very ill in hospital for about six weeks before her birth. But Chloe was born and she was a lovely bouncy, happy baby and everything was wonderful.

Nothing, nothing in the world could have prepared us for what was going to happen next. It was 26th November, 1991, in the evening, that she stopped breathing. It was a moment of distraction: Derek was on the phone, I was cooking supper, and when I went to look at her a few minutes later, I found her dead. Derek called an ambulance and we attempted to revive her before it came. Eventually it arrived and she was raced to St George's Hospital, Tooting, where she was put in Intensive Care.

It was awful when they were trying to get her heart going. It took a long time, probably about forty-five minutes, and a human being dies in three minutes if they don't get oxygen. So that in itself was amazing, that after forty-five minutes they were able to start her heart beating again. She was put on a life support machine and never breathed on her own again. She lived another seventeen hours, and they were the longest hours in my life. A second seemed like a day, a minute seemed like a year and an hour seemed like eternity. We didn't know what to do with ourselves. There are no words that can describe parents' feelings. She was our life. One minute we had a bouncy, healthy baby and the next minute the person our whole lives revolved around was dying. Our lives came to a grinding halt. We were unprepared and numb. We wanted to be with her, but the agony of seeing her was almost too much to bear. We were sick with shock and exhausted beyond belief. We had done everything for her in the past but now we found ourselves helpless and other people had taken over. We could not just pick our baby up, walk out of that place and give her a cuddle which we longed to do. Everything was alien to us and it was a struggle to take it in.

But it was in this situation that the Lord showed his compassion, which was amazing. I had always wanted Chloe baptised. Before she became ill Derek was indifferent to it and he hadn't wanted a big fuss but now he agreed and we decided she had to be baptised. Gradually it became obvious that we were going to lose her and as our hopes for her life faded we realised it was an ordeal we would have to live through. The chaplain was there and we had her baptised. Moments after the baptism I said to Derek, 'The Holy Spirit's here!' and I didn't know anything about the Holy Spirit. God's love for me was so incredible that he sent his Spirit down to comfort me at that time. I felt this amazing source of strength and peace.

Towards the end our nurse said she thought I should hold Chloe. I was frightened I'd hurt her. Then she said, 'I think she'd far rather be in your arms.' So I took her and she died in my arms. But before that happened, I felt God. I felt overwhelmed with his love and I felt held in his arms, as I was holding Chloe in mine. And the extraordinary thing is that I didn't really know that any of these things could happen. I wasn't a proper Christian at all, apart from going through the traditional motions, and yet that's when I knew that I'd had a physical experience of his love and light. There were tears, but no hysteria. The calmness came from him. I felt I had no right to hold her back and though my heart was breaking as I held her little hand I knew with certainty she was with Jesus and that Jesus himself had been longing to hold and care for her.

Then we left the hospital and we came home and we had no child. I was thrown into a pit of despair and my world was black: it was like I was suspended in a well of black ink. All around there was suffocating blackness; I couldn't look out of a window and feel joy, as part of me had died. Nothing could lift me, I was so, so sad.

We went to Florida for Christmas as had been planned. When we came back, I bumped into Susie Farley, a neighbour I had met at ante-natal classes. Of course I had no baby, and her little baby Harry was there and she asked where Chloe was, and I had to tell her. She was so kind. She was obviously very sad and asked me if I was a Christian. My words to her were that I didn't know if I was, if God could allow such things, yet all the time I knew I'd experienced his love. Susie asked me if I'd think of going to Alpha, a course at her church, Holy Trinity Brompton. I wouldn't have gone if she hadn't driven me there and introduced me to others. But the wonderful thing was that the moment my foot walked over the threshold of the room there, I felt the same feeling of light and joy and love that I'd known at the time of Chloe's death.

I never looked back after that moment. That was the only thing that lifted me. I went back again and completed the course. People were so kind. I suddenly knew there was the sky and there were birds in it and there was a rainbow and wonderful things around. There was something worth living for again. Derek couldn't believe the difference in me. He was very suspicious because he thought I was getting involved in some Moonie religious organisation and he thought he had to stamp it out, fast. I managed to persuade him to come on the next evening Alpha course. Very sweetly he said he'd come for me. For the first five weeks he was aggressive and used convincing arguments against becoming a Christian.

Then one day, halfway through the course, he was sitting in the barber's shop and looking at himself, and he prayed that God would come into his life. He now says that God answered immediately and that he felt the whole of the heavens rejoice as though a voice was saying, 'At long last! We've been waiting all your life for you to do this. Thank you for doing it!'

Our lives changed dramatically after that point. Derek resigned from his job, so we had almost a year together while he was unemployed. The Bible talks about putting us in a spacious place (eg Psalm 18:19) and God did. He gave us the space we needed to be ourselves and to build our faith. He has more than provided for us in every possible way. He has given us wonderful friends – far closer than we've ever had before – who pray for all parts of our lives consistently. In the same week that our second child, Freya, was born, Derek got the job he's in now which is just right for him. It was such a clear demonstration of God's perfect timing for our lives.

Every day I cry for Chloe. I still love her. Some months after she died I did ask the question 'Why?' because she seemed so perfect and it seemed such a waste. You always know when it's God replying because the answer is so powerful. I sensed him say, 'Chloe is much happier in heaven than she would ever have been on earth.' And I said, 'But I loved her so much, Lord. There was so much that I wanted to teach her, so much I wanted to show her.' He said to me, 'Now do you understand why you need to love me at least as much as you love Chloe? There is so much I want to teach and show you.'

Little Freya is the most lovely child and we delight in her. As Freya grows up we see how much she would have loved to have had a sister. She adores other children. Grief is not something you 'get over' like a bad cold, and the pain is something you learn to live with; it's the physical absence of the person you love which is the hardest thing to bear. But the Lord continues to be our strength. He has never yet failed us. He continues in his Spirit to heal and comfort us and we always arrive at a restored peacefulness once more. There is no secret to knowing his love. We only have to seek it. Through Chloe's death I knew what 'it' was all about and that in suffering I was growing up, literally overnight. Growing up is learning to accept God's will (sometimes it's hard to grow up). This for me was the moment of reckoning. I felt I had only half-lived. My spirit has been awakened and this was an aspect to my existing on this earth which I had never known before.

The Lord must not only have loved me beyond my understanding but I think he knew that once I knew and loved him, I would never turn back from his power on my life and my family. It has been too strong a force. I will never forget his goodness to me in my darkest hours. I was nothing before him and I would be nothing without him – he is the centre of my life.

11
Ministry

What makes Alpha so exciting is the work of the Holy
Spirit among us. It is his activity which transforms the
talks, the discussion groups, the Bible studies, pastoral
care, administration and every other aspect of Alpha.
The word 'ministry' is used in several different ways in
the New Testament and in the church today. In one
sense, ministry includes everything done in a church and
every aspect of an Alpha course. John Wimber has
defined ministry as 'meeting the needs of others on the
basis of God's resources'. The New Bible Dictionary
points out, 'In its earliest form the Christian ministry is
charismatic, ie it is a spiritual gift or supernatural
endowment, whose exercise witnesses to the presence of
the Holy Spirit in the Church.'[25] In this chapter, however
I am using a narrower sense of the word: when
we specifically pray for others in the power of the
Holy Spirit.

One of the most astonishing stories in the Old
Testament is the account of Moses and the people of
Israel crossing the Red Sea. When they came to the sea
God said to Moses, 'Raise your staff and stretch out your
hand over the sea to divide the water so that the
Israelites can go through the sea on dry ground' (Ex
14:16). God was asking Moses to do his part while
promising to do his own part, by dividing the sea. I

wonder what went through Moses' mind at that moment. He would have felt an idiot if he had stretched out his hand and God had not divided the sea. He may have thought it would have been much easier if God had just divided the sea without involving him. But as is often the case in the Bible, there is a co-operation between us and God. God allows us to be involved in his plans. We do our part and God does his. Our part is relatively simple. God's is not so easy.

Moses took a step of faith and 'stretched out his hand' (Ex 14: 21). God responded and '…all that night the Lord drove the sea back with a strong east wind and turned it into dry land. The waters were divided, and the Israelites went through the sea on dry ground, with a wall of water on their right and on their left' (Ex 14:21-22).

God has not changed. This story reminds us that when we do what he asks us to do, he does what he has promised to do. As we pray for others he sends his Holy Spirit to transform lives. This might be prayer for others to be filled with the Spirit, to receive some gift (eg the gift of tongues), or prayer for healing.

Ministry values

The most fundamental thing here is to recognise that this is a ministry of the Holy Spirit. It is not our power but his. What God asked Moses to do was very simple; he did not have to shout or dance or leap about. Likewise, we encourage our leaders to be totally natural and simply to be themselves, to take a step of faith and stretch out their hands and ask God to send his Spirit. The rest is up to him. Sometimes I look around while ministry is happening and see leaders or helpers stepping out in faith for the first time in this area. There is often an expression of astonishment, bewilderment and joy on their faces as they see how God uses them.

Sometimes when we see the extraordinary work of the Spirit we may be tempted to look at the fruit rather than the vine. But we are to keep looking to Jesus. Jesus taught his disciples not to be sidetracked in any way from the most important issues. When the seventy-two returned joyfully from the places they had been sent to minister to and said, 'Lord, even the demons submit to us in your name' (Lk 10:17), Jesus replied, 'I saw Satan fall like lightning from heaven. I have given you authority to trample on snakes and scorpions and to overcome all the power of the enemy; nothing will harm you. However, do not rejoice that the spirits submit to you, but rejoice that your names are written in heaven' (Lk 10:18-20).

Secondly, and of equal importance, all ministry must take place under the authority of the Bible. The Spirit of God and the written word of God will never be in conflict. They complement each other. God will never do or say anything which is inconsistent with his revealed will and character in the Bible. Because the word and the Spirit go hand in hand we encourage our leaders to be steeped in the biblical truths and promises as part of ministry. It is the truth that sets people free (Jn 8:32). I ask people to make sure they know where key passages are that relate to the kinds of needs which emerge as we pray for people. For example, some of the passages we often use are the following: Psalm 51 (repentance), Psalm 91 (fear), Philippians 4:6-7 (anxiety), Psalm 37:5 (guidance), 1 Corinthians 10:13 (temptation).

Our third main concern in ministry is the dignity of the individual: if we love people we will show them respect. This means first that confidentiality is assured. If people tell us confidential matters about their lives they need to be assured it will go no further. It will not be 'shared for prayer' or discussed at helpers' meetings.

Next, we must affirm rather than condemn. We don't say, 'It's your fault,' if people are not healed, or suggest that it was because they did not have enough faith. Jesus never told an individual that it was their lack of faith that stopped them being healed. Occasionally he upbraided his disciples for their lack of faith (and we may need to ask ourselves whether we lack faith) but he never condemned the sick person in this way. We should not place additional burdens on anyone, let alone those who are sick. If they are not healed we never suggest that they should believe that they are. Rather we give them the freedom to come back and pray again. This kind of prayer should always be done in a low-key way and any super-spirituality and unnatural intensity should be avoided at all costs.

The fourth value is harmonious relationships. Jesus prayed for his disciples, 'May they be brought to complete unity to let the world know that you sent me and have loved them even as you have loved me' (Jn 17:23). The unity of the people of God was a high priority on Jesus' agenda and it should be so on ours. A lack of unity, love and forgiveness on the team hinders the work of the Spirit and is a terrible example to those on Alpha. It is vital that each group's leaders and helpers find time to pray together, as prayer is the most effective way of rooting out petty irritations. We make it a rule on Alpha never to criticise another denomination, another Christian church or a Christian leader. We try to support and encourage one another constantly. I discourage anyone from making negative remarks about another team member even as a joke. We are extremely careful during the entertainment on the weekend away not to allow any skits which have even a hint of cynicism or are in any way negative. This may seem excessive, but we have found in the past that even the most off-the-cuff comment can have a detrimental effect.

Our fifth value is the vital importance of the body of Christ. The Christian community is the place where long-term healing and spiritual growth take place under the protective umbrella of the authority of the church. Hence, we stress that each person should try to find a group where they can grow and develop. Leaders and helpers are responsible for helping each person under their care to find such a group.

A model for ministry

As well as having values on which our ministry is based, it is important to have a model about which we are confident so that all the theory may be put into practice and not left simply as theory. Over the years on Alpha we have developed a model which is not the only way nor even necessarily the best way, but it is one which we have found God works through and is simple enough for anyone to use and to feel confident in doing so.

When we pray for individuals we do so ideally with a team of two or, at most, three. Sometimes, for example on the Sunday morning of the weekend on the Holy Spirit, there are so many people who want to be prayed for that there are not enough leaders and helpers to go around. On these occasions we may only have one person praying for each individual. If this is the case we make it an absolute rule that men should pray for men and women for women. Often during these times of prayer the Holy Spirit brings out aspects of people's lives which are very personal and intimate. Also, at these moments a very strong bond may be formed between the person praying and the one being prayed for, and if the person is of the opposite sex there is a danger of misunderstanding and a misreading of signals. If there is more than one person praying then at least one should be of the same sex as the person being prayed for.

At these prayer times one person should take the lead and should be seen to do so with the prayerful help of the others. If more than one person is attempting to lead there is a danger that signals will be confused. For example, it is not helpful if one is saying, 'Hold on,' and the other is saying, 'Let go!'

As far as possible it is good to find a relaxed and private place to pray. If there are a lot of people in the room, it is important that others around cannot hear everything that is being said, to avoid embarrassment for the person receiving prayer. In other situations, I have sometimes seen the most inappropriate raising of voices and even shouting, to the intense discomfort of the person receiving prayer.

We usually begin by asking the person what they would like prayer for. We then take time to sort out difficulties in understanding, belief and assurance. Often there is a need for repentance and forgiveness, both receiving forgiveness and forgiving others. Lack of repentance and forgiveness are major stumbling blocks to the work of the Holy Spirit in our lives.

Sometimes at this point it becomes clear that the person is not yet a Christian. Each member of the team needs to be confident that they can lead someone to Christ. I would usually go through the booklet *Why Jesus?* briefly and then ask the person if they would like to pray the prayer in the back right then or whether they would rather go away and think about it (it is important always to give people a let out which is equally acceptable so that they do not feel pressurised into doing something for which they are not ready). If they say they would like to do so right then, I would pray for them briefly and then encourage them to read the prayer out loud, slowly and thoughtfully, adding anything they wish. After this I would pray another prayer for them asking the Spirit of God to come and fill them.

Others may already be Christians but have never really experienced God or the power of the Holy Spirit. We need to encourage them with truth through scriptural illustrations and promises. We need to deal with any difficulties they may have. They may say, 'Am I quite ready?' to which the answer, in one sense, is that we will never be totally ready. Some say, 'I'm unworthy,' to which the answer is, 'We are all unworthy. That is why Jesus died for us.' Most often there is a feeling that it could 'never happen to me'. For example, they might want to receive the gift of tongues but say, 'I could never speak in another language.' Again, we need to raise faith by pointing to the promises of God (1 Cor 14:2, 4, 14; Mt 7:11). One aspect of faith is taking a promise of God and daring to believe it.

As we pray for the person we stay facing them and, if they have no objection, we lay hands on them. Then, keeping our eyes open, we ask the Holy Spirit to come. We welcome him when we see signs of his working and wait on God as we pray for further directions. It is important not to pray 'around-the-world' prayers, ie going off in every conceivable direction because you are running out of things to pray. Rather we should silently ask God what he wants to do or say, how he wants to encourage the person and what gifts he wants to impart.

On the Alpha weekend we often pray for people to receive the gift of tongues (see *Questions of Life*, pp139-147). This is not because it is the most important gift but because the Alpha course is a beginners' course and the gift of tongues is a beginners' gift. It is neither the mark of being a Christian, nor a necessary sign of being filled with the Spirit. The gift of tongues does not elevate you into a spiritual elite, nor is it indeed necessary to speak in tongues. However, both in the Bible and in experience it is often the first obviously supernatural gift of the Spirit which people receive. Our understanding of the

New Testament is that it is available to all Christians and therefore we can pray with great confidence for them to receive.

The small group is the place to deal with people's fears and hesitations. I would ask those in the small group if anyone has had any experience in this area, good or bad. If they have, I ask them to speak about it. Usually there is someone (it might be a leader or a helper) who speaks in tongues themselves and is able to explain what it is and what the benefits are.

When praying for people to receive the gift of tongues I have found the greatest barrier is a psychological one – making the first sound. Once a person has made the first sound the rest usually follows quite naturally. In order to help people to get over this barrier I explain this difficulty and suggest that they start by copying what I or one of the other prayers is saying. Then I start to speak in tongues slowly so that they can follow. Once they have made the first sound they are usually away praying in their own language. I encourage them to try and concentrate on their relationship with God and try, as far as possible, not to be self-conscious. Rather they should concentrate on praising God with the new language he has given to them.

After we have finished praying for a person to be filled with the Spirit, receive a gift, be healed or whatever it is, we should ask what is happening and what they sense God is saying to them. We should encourage them to hold on to the promises of God, and warn them against possible increased temptation. We don't believe it is possible that 'nothing has happened'. They may not be aware especially at the time but when we ask the Spirit of God to come, he has promised to come. They may not know the difference until hours or even days later but something will have happened. We need to encourage them to keep in touch and to let us know how they are getting on. Of course, it is not a one-off experience; they need to go on being filled with the Spirit (Eph 5:18).

Opportunities for ministry

Much of the ministry takes place on the weekend away. The early part of the weekend is usually spent in raising faith and dealing with difficulties. On Friday night we have a very short talk on the Holy Spirit based around John 15:26. I try to keep this short and light-hearted as people are often exhausted after a busy week and a long journey.

On the Saturday morning we look at 'Who is the Holy Spirit?' and 'What does the Holy Spirit do?' (see *Questions of Life*, Chapters 8 and 9). Then at 12.15 pm we go into the usual small groups and look at 1 Corinthians 12: 1-8. This gives people an opportunity to discuss some of the most obviously supernatural gifts of the Spirit.

On Saturday afternoon there is an opportunity to ask for counselling with an experienced (though not professionally trained) counsellor. We put up a list of the counsellors and people can sign up for this if they have questions they want to ask, difficulties they would like help in thinking through, or if they would like to receive prayer for some area in their lives. During these sessions some give their lives to Christ, some are filled with the Spirit; others receive new gifts.

On the Saturday evening (at 5.00 pm) I speak on 'How can I be filled with the Spirit?' (Chapter 10 in *Questions of Life*). At the end of the talk I explain that I am going to invite the Holy Spirit to come and fill those who would like to be filled and give the gift of tongues to those who would like to receive. I ask everyone to stand, to close their eyes and to hold out their hands in front of them if they would like to receive. Our body language often expresses what we feel, and holding out our hands is what we do when we are about to receive a gift: thus it is a sign between the person and God that they would like to receive.

I then pray a prayer which others can echo in their hearts. It is a prayer of repentance, faith and commitment to Jesus Christ. I then ask the Holy Spirit to come and fill all those who have invited him into their lives. We then wait and watch as he comes and does what he wants to do. It is always different and always exciting to see God at work in our midst. Sometimes the manifestations of the Spirit are obvious. Some are so overwhelmed by the Holy Spirit they find it hard to remain standing. Others are so deeply moved by the love of God that tears run down their faces. Some are so filled with joy that they burst out laughing. For others there is no outward manifestation but a work of God in their hearts is bringing a sense of peace and a deep assurance of his presence and love. All should be encouraged, and no one should be made to feel guilty, second-rate or rushed along against their will.

At the end of the course I send out questionnaires asking (a) whether people were Christians before the course and (b) how they would describe themselves now. If there is a change I ask when that change occurred. For many the decisive moment is the Saturday evening of the weekend. Here are five examples of how people at one Alpha weekend described their experiences:

– 'After the talk about "How can I be filled with the Holy Spirit?" we all stood up and the Holy Spirit came into the room. I knew that God was real so I asked Jesus into my heart and he's been there ever since … I have suddenly got a whole new outlook on life.'

– The change had occurred 'during the Saturday evening talks/services. I was filled with the Holy Spirit. I felt a white sheet wipe me clean then a strong rush of

light came through me from my waist and up out of my
head – the feeling made me lift my arms in the air.'

– 'I had been a Christian in my head only. This
changed on the Alpha weekend when God spoke to me
personally. I asked him for his Holy Spirit and the result
was electrifying.'

– Someone who had been involved in the New Age
movement at the start of the course said that the change
occurred on the Saturday evening when 'the Spirit shook
me from head to foot'.

– 'I had a phenomenal experience of the Holy Spirit
cleansing me, freeing me, releasing my sins and loving
me; giving me a fresh plateau, a new life. It was the 20th
February when I really started to *live*!'

After the Saturday evening we respond to God in
songs of thanksgiving and praise. Sometimes we will
sing in tongues. I explain that singing in tongues together
is different from all speaking in tongues together.
Speaking in tongues without interpretation is a private
activity which should only be done on our own. Singing
in tongues is a corporate activity of praise and worship
to God, co-ordinated by the Spirit of God. On occasions,
it has been one of the most beautiful and almost angelic
sounds I have ever heard. It is also a golden opportunity
for people to receive the gift of tongues as they begin to
sing praises to God in the language he gives them.

We do not usually pray for individuals on the
Saturday night unless they specifically ask for prayer
(which some often do at this stage). Instead, after supper
we have an evening of entertainment organised by
someone on the team. This is a good time for people to
relax and unwind by performing or spectating. We invite
participation by anyone who would like to contribute. It
is usually a mixture of musical contributions, joke telling
and amusing sketches. The quality is sometimes a little
mixed, but it always involves lots of laughter. We try to

ensure that the whole evening is as positive and upbuilding as possible.

On Sunday morning at 9.45 am we meet in small groups briefly to make sure that everyone is happy and to discuss any difficulties or questions which may have arisen on the Saturday and at 10.30 am we have our informal communion service. We begin with praise and prayer. Then we have a talk on 'How can I make the most of the rest of my life?' (see *Questions of Life*, Chapter 15). At the end I invite people to give every part of their lives to God, 'to offer your bodies as living sacrifices' (Rom 12:1). This is the appropriate response to all that God has done for us. In some circles it would be described as a 'wholeheartedness talk'. It might be argued that this should come before the talk on being filled with the Spirit; that as we open all the doors of our house he fills each part with his Spirit. I am sure there is something in this, but the movement in Scripture is from him to us. He blesses us out of sheer grace and mercy and we respond by giving ourselves to him out of love. When we begin to understand and experience the love of God for us as we are filled with his Spirit, our only appropriate response is to give everything we have to him.

After the talk, we greet one another with a sign of peace. At this stage we have a few moments' break and move around greeting one another and chatting briefly. By this time there is a lot to talk and laugh about and there is usually quite a din! After the peace we sing a song of praise. We have an offering which covers the cost of those who could not afford to pay for all or part of the weekend. One of the exciting things about these weekends is that we almost always end up with exactly the amount in the offering to cover those we have subsidised. People are learning right from the start that in the Christian family those who have more should help those who have less.

I then explain the communion service (along the lines of *Questions of Life*, pp 228-229). This is a good opportunity to teach about the central service of the Christian faith. We then invite anyone who knows and loves Jesus Christ to receive communion, should they wish, regardless of their denomination or background. We pass round the bread and the wine, asking those who do not wish to receive for any reason to pass it on to their neighbour. Many comment on the beautiful simplicity and unity in this, and some experience God's love for the first time as they relax and receive the bread and wine.

After the communion is over I invite people to stand and again ask the Holy Spirit to come and work among us. After waiting for a short time I ask members of the team to begin praying with those who would like prayer. At this stage it is important for each member of the team to have the courage and confidence to go and pray for those in their groups along the lines I have suggested earlier in this chapter. This prayer goes on for some time. I usually end the service with a song and the blessing at around 1.00 pm, but prayer for some continues while the rest of us go to lunch.

After lunch at 2.00 pm we gather for five minutes to give thanks to our hosts and deal with any final administrative matters. We arrange to meet at the evening service (for those who are able to come), and reserve all the front seats of the church for those who have been on the weekend. For many it is their first time in the church. There is always a sense of great excitement and celebration on these occasions. The ministry of the Spirit continues and some are filled with the Spirit and receive gifts during or after the evening service.

Another excellent opportunity for those on the course to learn about ministry is the healing evening (*Questions of Life*, Chapter 13) which occurs during week nine. The evening follows the normal pattern until after coffee at

9.00 pm. On this evening we do not then go into small groups: rather, we stay together for a practical healing session.

At this point we outline the model of healing prayer which we follow (*Questions of Life*, pp 213-214). We then explain that God sometimes gives words of knowledge (1 Cor 12:8) which point out whom God wants us to pray for and which are also an aid to faith in this area. We have found that people receive these words in various ways. Some may get a mental picture of the part of the body which God wants to heal. Some will merely receive an impression, and others may sense that they hear or see words. We have found that one of the most common ways we receive words of knowledge is by what we call 'a sympathy pain': someone senses pain in their body, which they know is not really theirs.

Simon Dixon, who has since become our organist, had a stabbing pain when he moved or when he was touched around his jaw or neck. It had been very painful for a year and a half and he had been told it couldn't be cured. He had lots of medical tests, but the doctors did not know what was wrong. They thought it might be a brain tumour. He was finally diagnosed as having auricular neuralgia. He was on a lot of drugs and at times his vision was affected. A woman in our congregation called Emma had felt a pain in her jaw which she thought must be a sympathy pain and therefore a word of knowledge. As a result, after prayer for healing, he was sufficiently cured to come off the drugs and after further prayer was totally healed. Since then he has been perfectly healthy.

At the end of this explanation we ask if anyone senses that they have any words of knowledge. Usually there are many (often received by those who are relatively new Christians who have never had the disadvantage of being told that God does not speak to his people today). They expect God to speak to them and he does. We write down all the words of knowledge. Sometimes we go through the list one by one asking people to identify themselves (providing, of course, the condition described is not one likely to cause embarrassment). On other occasions we simply ask all those who want to respond to stand at the same time.

Next, we ask one of those who have responded (if they are willing) to be prayed for in public. We then get two or three experienced people to pray for the person to provide a model of how to pray for healing. Whoever is leading the evening explains exactly what is happening.

Then we arrange for two or three people to pray for each of those who have responded to the words of knowledge. We try to get those who have had the particular words of knowledge to pray for those who responded to them. By this time almost everyone on the course is involved in the ministry. If there are any not involved we suggest they join a group to watch and learn from what is going on.

It is very exciting to see those who have only recently come to Christ praying, often with great faith, for others in a similar position. We have seen some remarkable healings on these evenings and we nearly always see conversions as well. One teenager called Bill brought his mother Judy, who was not a Christian, on an Alpha course. She had enjoyed the course but was still quite sceptical about the healing evening. That night there was a word of knowledge for a shoulder injury. She responded and was healed. She said afterwards, 'Many things had happened to me during Alpha that were answers to prayer which I had tried to explain away as co-incidences, but it was the healing that made me realise that I could no longer say it was a coincidence. I prayed in my heart and made a commitment.' Since then she has been a helper on a number of Alpha courses, being increasingly involved in the organisation and administration.

The ministry of the Spirit is crucial to Alpha – without it, it would not really be an Alpha course. We have found that time and again God has honoured simple requests for him to send his Spirit among us. Amazing and profound changes always occur in people's lives as a result. We are continuing to see people give their lives to Christ, be filled with the Spirit, get excited about Jesus and bring their friends to the next course.

Testimony 6

PAUL AND CLINTON COWLEY

12
Paul and Clinton Cowley

Paul Cowley didn't speak to his teenage son Clinton for six years. Having divorced Clinton's mother when his child was three, he gradually lost contact over the years. Then, four years ago, Paul joined the Alpha course at Holy Trinity Brompton after visiting the church at the recommendation of a friend. During Alpha, he gave his life to Jesus Christ. Meanwhile, Clinton was getting increasingly involved in the drugs scene near his home in Cambridgeshire. Here, Paul, and Clinton – who is now seventeen years old – tell how God has brought them back together again and how Alpha has had a remarkable impact on both of their lives.

Paul

I was born in Manchester. I left home when I was fifteen because I was a bit of a rebel and my mum and dad couldn't really cope. Soon afterwards, my father divorced my mother. When I asked him why he had divorced, he said he had only been married because I was there and when I left home, there was nothing left of their relationship. So they split up.

During the next five years, Paul became involved with a group of skinheads and built up a criminal record, mostly for stealing cars and joyriding. At the age of twenty, he was accepted by the army and soon grew to love it.

153

Around that time, I met Lynn, who became my girlfriend. After my training, I was posted to Germany and we had to make a decision either to get married or to separate because she couldn't go with me as a girlfriend. She had to be a wife. So we got married.

A year later, we had a little boy – Clinton. We were living in Bergen in Germany, on the north-east side near the border with Russia, and I was throwing myself into my work. I was hungry to get promotion and I didn't care who I stood on or what I did. The only thing I wanted to do was get out of being a non-ranker to get some rank – which I did quite quickly.

The marriage broke up three years later and the couple were divorced. Paul accepts this was because of his single-minded ambition in the army and 'a variety of different relationships with women'.

The years went by. Occasionally I would organise for Clinton to fly out to where I was so that we could have a week or weekend together. I had a variety of different relationships with women through that time, and he would come out and meet them.

If I was back in England we would sometimes have a few days together between my flights, but it wasn't a priority. I also visited my mother and father when I was in the country, but I didn't tell my father that I had seen my mother, because he would get really angry. When I saw my mum I didn't mention my dad either. In between that, I actually had to try and see Clinton as well. Every time I saw him it would be great, but when I left he would break down and cry. He wanted to be with me but I couldn't cope with that.

Soon after this, Paul met an art student called Amanda while working in Cyprus and the two began sharing a home together.

During that time, my mother became ill with cancer. I was posted in Warwickshire at the time and Amanda and I had a house there. So my mother came and lived in our house. Not long afterwards she died. It was quite a blow really because I was just getting a relationship back with her. I was really angry, but Amanda was amazing. She guided me and took control.

While we were sorting through my mum's stuff, I found a Bible – the Good News Bible. I looked inside it and there were lots of passages marked. There was also a name and telephone number. We rang the number and spoke to a lady who turned out to be a friend of my mother's from Manchester. I went to visit her and she told me that my mother had become a Christian about two years before she died. My mum had never said anything about it at all. That blew my socks off really, because my mum was a hard Northern woman and quite volatile. I just couldn't take on board the idea of her being a Christian...

Occasionally Clinton would come and stay with us – he has always got on well with Amanda – but gradually he stopped coming and we lost contact. I have to admit that Amanda was a far greater priority to me than he was at that time.

Paul then left the army and became fitness director of a men's health club in Mayfair.

Amanda really encouraged me to write to Clinton, which I found really difficult because I never got any replies back. She said, 'You need to keep writing. You need to keep that channel open.' So I would write. I would be a bit cynical about it, but I would keep writing. I never got any replies at all.

Soon afterwards, Amanda and I were visiting some friends in Rye, on the south coast, for the weekend. On the Sunday morning we went for a walk along the seafront and I suddenly said to her, 'I want to go to church.' Amanda nearly fell over and said, 'What do you mean, you want to go to church?' I said, 'Well, I just feel that I would like to go to church.' She said, 'You're probably going to be really bored.' But we went – and I was really bored.

For the next eight months, Paul visited a wide variety of churches around London, but settled upon Holy Trinity Brompton.

Then someone suggested the Alpha course and I thought, 'If I was trying to be a mechanic I would go to maintenance classes.' This seemed to be a course for people who wanted to find out about God. So I read the literature and we attended the course. We were put in a group with a chap called Geoff Wilmot and I am sure I was Geoff Wilmot's nightmare. I must have asked every question. Amanda told me to be quiet on lots of occasions, but I knew nothing and I wanted to know everything. I wanted the whole 2,000 years of Christianity explained to me! He was great – so patient.

So Amanda and I did that course together. After that, we were asked to come back to help on the next course, so we did. Before the end of the second course, I stopped thinking about the 'head' stuff and concentrated more on putting it in my heart.

I remembered reading in the Bible where Jesus says, 'You have to come to me as a child.' So I thought, 'What does that mean – a child?' I thought about Clinton and how he would always trust me. So I thought, 'I am going to come to Jesus as a child.' So I gave my life to Christ. I gave him my heart and I committed myself to him.

Amanda, who had done something similar at the age of thirteen but had never followed it through, did the same a little bit later. As soon as I allowed God to 'get me', my whole concept on life completely changed. It was like the scales were removed from my eyes. I had a different perspective on life completely.

Paul and Amanda were married soon afterwards and began praying with their church group that Paul would be reconciled

with Clinton, to whom he continued to write regularly. It was
two years before Clinton was to make contact.

I got a phone call in my office out of the blue: 'I want
to come and see you, Dad.'

'OK, when?'

'Today.'

So I said, 'When today?'

He said, 'I'll be at King's Cross at seven o'clock.'

I had not seen him or spoken to him for six years.

It was a Tuesday night – the night of our home group
(by then we were running one of our own), so I told
Amanda that I was going to need a lot of prayer for this.
She got the whole group praying for this meeting at
seven o'clock. I turned up at King's Cross and saw him.
I had left a little cute boy but now this 'thug' was
walking towards me. He had dark glasses on and a small
suitcase. It frightened the life out of me, really.

It was quite hard to talk at first. We went out that night
for something to eat, just me and Clint. I took him home
and we talked and we talked and we talked. We talked
about Jesus. We talked about his life. We talked about a
suicide attempt. We just talked about all sorts.

I managed to get him a job through a contact that I
had. So he started work there which put him in a suit
which meant he had to tidy himself up.

I was praying a lot for Clinton to go on Alpha, but I
didn't want to push it. In the end, one day as we were
getting ready to go to a Sunday service, he said, 'Oh, I'll
come with you.' That was about seven months ago. He
came and he sat in church. Then he came again. He went
from the hard aggressive stance, to the lighter one, to
standing up, to singing. Then he said, 'I might do the
Alpha course, Dad.'

I said, 'OK, that would be great.' I was singing and
dancing inside!

One night at home, half way through the course, he

said, 'I want you to talk to me a bit more about Jesus and all that stuff.' So we did, Amanda and I. In the end we prayed together on the settee and he gave his life to Christ there and then, which was amazing. Then *his* life started to change. He started to pray for things. His drugs are now out the window. He has stopped smoking and is on a management career course where he works.

Clinton

I was born in 1978 in Stockport. I lived there for about six months and then moved to Germany with my dad and my mum. They split up when I was about three. I vaguely remember bits of it. I just remember arguments and things. My mum and I moved into a friend's house in Chester. Then my mum met my stepdad. They started living together after about a year. I didn't get on with him at all. I felt that he wasn't my dad. I saw my real dad once or twice a year when he was in the country. We moved to Cambridge when I was about ten years old.

Both my mum and stepdad were career people, so I used to go to a childminder after school for two or three hours, until about five or six o'clock when they finished work. I didn't like going to childminders at all. So I used to be quite lippy and cheeky with them.

When I went to secondary school at thirteen, I started getting into fights with people. I got involved in burning stuff down, smashing stuff, fighting all the time, starting gang fights, bunking off school.

Clinton began dabbling in drugs – dope, speed, and acid – and was soon dealing in them to pay for his habit. Within a short time, his life revolved around the drug culture.

Drugs protect people. There is no list of rules, but you just learn things as you go along. If you don't rub people up the wrong way, and you buy a lot and you sell a lot and you always pay your bills and you never say where you got it from – you will go very far and have no problems.

I was about fifteen or sixteen when I started doing Ecstasy, and that was really good fun. I got a motorbike then and we decided to start selling at clubs. I dealt in everything and anything people wanted. The trouble with drugs is that they build you up to a certain level, but then you need something else, so you take another tablet. Then it builds you up again, but you never get what you are looking for, ever. I became a drop-out. I didn't bother about school. I didn't bother about anything.

Clinton saw very little of his mother and left notes at home to say he was staying elsewhere. Then, one day, he looked at himself and became concerned that he was becoming more and more of a drug abuser. Later that day, he bumped into his mother in a shop...

I was walking to the shop. It was sunny, but I was off my head with the drugs. I was just walking all over the place and knocked over a stand in the shop. Just as I was walking out, my mum walked up to me, tapped me on the shoulder and said, 'Who do you think you are?'

I said, 'What do you mean?'

'You haven't been home for days. You are sixteen years old. What do you think you are doing?'

It just blew my mind – I couldn't deal with it. Then she started crying in front of me. She said, 'You're turning out just like your father.' I didn't know my dad that well. Mum had always kept my dad's colourful past secret from me.

'Why are you being like this?' she said.

I said, 'I have done something really bad, but I can't tell you what I am doing.' I was so ashamed at that point. More ashamed than at any time in my life.

I just looked at her and she was crying. My mum is not an emotional person. She does not cry often, but she was

crying in front of me, and I just felt like all the guilt in the
world was on my shoulders. I said, 'I can't tell you.' She
cried and she hugged me. She said, 'I think you should
see your father because he was quite a wild one in his
youth.' My mum had always been against me seeing my
father before.

I said, 'All right, then.' I wanted her out of my way. I
was getting really emotional. I wasn't a crier. I was a bit
of a toughie but I could feel a tear in my eye.

*Clinton came close to suicide that night. He recalls, 'I just
sat there and said to the sky, "If there is somebody out there,
then you had better help me now because I am going to die
soon from an overdose or something."' Next morning, his
mother phoned him at a friend's house and gave him his
father's telephone number.*

I rang the number from my friend's house. My dad,
who lived in London, said, 'Do you want to come to
London?' I said, 'All right, then.' He said, 'Today?' So I
said, 'OK.' I just got on the train and listened to my rave
music all the way to London. I was at the point where
nothing mattered. Nothing mattered at all.

I didn't think much when I saw him. I recognised him
when he came nearer. He held me and I felt very uneasy
about that. He said, 'Do you want to go out for
something to eat?' All night he was saying to me,
'What's wrong?'

I met Amanda, Dad's wife, that night. We went over to
the flat and she came over and hugged me and I was
very uneasy about that. I didn't know that they had been
praying for three years for me to come back. For me it
was just a really small event.

For them it must have been amazing.

The next day we went to lunch and my dad said, 'Is it
drugs?' He is quite open like that. I said, 'Yes.' Then I
started crying and the whole lot came out. We were in a
coffee shop in Maida Vale and I told him everything.

Clinton settled in London with his father and stepmother, where he started working at a job found for him by his father.

Dad kept saying to me, 'You should go to Alpha.' I said, 'No! No!' Then finally, I just said, 'All right, I will do it.' I didn't turn up for a few talks. Basically I was not really interested in it at all. I used to come and fall asleep in the talks.

On the Alpha weekend, I got absolutely legless. I went to the beach at about one o'clock in the morning with all the young people. I told my group leader, Bill, about my life and I was really crying, telling him that I didn't know why I was on an Alpha course and going to church. I felt an immense guilt because I was starting to get my old self back. I was starting to realise what I had really done to some people, like beating them up and ruining their lives with drugs. Bill kept saying to me that I could be forgiven and I just kept feeling that I could never be forgiven for the stuff that I had done. I just felt so ashamed.

One night I came home and told my dad I had had enough of work and that was it. I ended up crying again. I had cried twice in a week and I didn't know what was going on. Dad said, 'Should we pray about it?' I said, 'All right, then.' I thought he was going to say a quick grace or something. Amanda and Dad sat next to me on the settee and put their hands on me. I was in such a state that I just thought, 'Stuff it. Whatever you think that you can do for me, then do it – because if it works then great.' I thought it was going to be a quick prayer: 'Lord, take this pain away from him. Amen.' But it was a really long prayer asking God to forgive me and come into my life. It was really nice. I didn't really say anything myself. I just felt really easy. I got up and just felt better. I have never really said that this is the day that I became a Christian – but I think it was. I did Alpha again. I turned up this time, but still ended up getting drunk on the weekend. I listened to all the talks.

I have been getting to know God more over the weeks and months. I am 100% Christian now: I still have my difficulties, like everybody does. I still have my temptations, but I am getting so much stronger.

When I took drugs I lost everything. I lost my family, I lost my friends, I lost my home, every penny I had, my decency and my respect. The whole lot. I had to start all over again. That is what I have been doing for the last eleven months. God has totally transformed my life. I've been home three or four times in the last eleven months. They can see I have changed, although they haven't said anything.

I know God has forgiven me now. I pray constantly. I have to pray to live because I can't do without it. My relationship with my dad is very, very strong. We have worked through a lot of stuff. I have completely forgiven him.

Appendix A
Alpha Talk Scheme

The fifteen talks which make up the Alpha course are:

1. Christianity: Boring, Untrue and Irrelevant?
2. Who Is Jesus?
3. Why Did Jesus Die?
4. How Can I Be Sure of My Faith?
5. Why and How Should I Read the Bible?
6. Why and How Do I Pray?
7. How Does God Guide Us?
8. Who Is the Holy Spirit?
9. What Does the Holy Spirit Do?
10. How Can I Be Filled with the Spirit?
11. How Can I Resist Evil?
12. Why and How Should We Tell Others?
13. Does God Heal Today?
14. What About the Church?
15. How Can I Make the Most of the Rest of My Life?

Talk 1 is given at the celebration supper at the end of the course. Talks 8, 9, 10 and 15 are given at the weekend away. The best time for the weekend is half way through the course, but the date is flexible. If it comes later then the talk scheme needs to be adjusted accordingly. Whenever the weekend falls it is helpful to give Talk 11, *How Can I Resist Evil?*, directly afterwards even if it means the sequence of the talks changes slightly. This is because we have found this subject very relevant at this point.

Appendix B
Administration
by Philippa Pearson Miles

On an Alpha course there is a lot of hard work behind
the scenes and every job is vitally important. We aim to
get everything 100% right. Guests who come on the
course will see that every effort has been made and that
everything is run in an efficient way.

Some of this chapter will only apply to larger courses,
where the first thing the course leader should do is to
appoint an administrator.

Set a date

Make sure that your Alpha course does not overlap with
anything that will keep people from coming, eg
Christmas, Easter and summer holidays. Remember to
allow enough time for the supper parties at the end of
the course and the three training sessions. If you are
doing a Daytime Alpha (see Appendix C) then tie in
your course with the school term and include a break for
half term. We suggest you do not book the weekend
away over the half-term period.

Prepare brochure/letter

Prepare an attractive brochure with all the relevant
details and feel free to reproduce the Alpha logo.

Alternatively, produce a simple letter which sets out all the dates with a tear-off slip at the bottom. It is also possible to order four-colour customised brochures from the Alpha Office at Holy Trinity Brompton.

Inviting your team

First, contact the home group leaders of the church and ask them to suggest people whom they know who would be good Alpha leaders and helpers. It is vital to get the right people (see Chapter 3 – *Practicalities*). It is important to emphasise commitment to the course, because if the leaders are not consistent in coming then there is no reason why anybody else should come either.

Emphasise that their commitment is not just for ten weeks but also for three training nights, social evenings with their group, follow-up after the course has finished, getting members into a home group and integrating them into the church. Insist that all leaders and helpers come to the training sessions. If they are unable to come, ask them to listen to the tape. Even if some of your team have helped on several Alpha courses, they should come to every training session of every course. Even if one of your leaders has been leading small groups for twenty years or so, stress that Alpha small groups are very different. Ask the leaders and helpers to commit themselves to pray for every member of their group.

Arranging leadership of groups

This can be a very long task, so allow plenty of time. Be firm with your team, emphasising that everyone should be willing to do anything from leading to washing-up.

Arrange groups primarily by age and think carefully about the dynamics of the group: the balance of characters, social backgrounds, professions etc. It is also good to select a team from the same home group so that there can be continuity for the guests after the course, though this may not always work in practice. It is better to put together a team who will work well with one another. If you can, try to allocate a specific person in each group to look after the administration for their group, preferably someone who is gifted in that area and who can definitely come to the administration/prayer meetings every week.

Advertising

The most effective way of advertising an Alpha course is through the celebration supper at the end of the course. This provides an opportunity for guests to invite their friends to see what they have been doing for the last ten weeks. (The supper is discussed in more detail later on in this Appendix.)

The two Sundays prior to the beginning of the Alpha course should be designated 'Alpha Sundays'. At Holy Trinity the first Sunday is a regular service with a testimony and a slot advertising Alpha. The second Sunday is a guest service which is designed especially for church members to invite their friends and family. This service is low-key and the sermon is evangelistic and challenging. Again Alpha would be advertised and a testimony heard. Alpha brochures and complimentary copies of *Why Jesus?* are given to everyone at the end. An Alpha team, wearing Alpha sweatshirts, is available afterwards to answer questions.

Suggested guest service timetable

6.30 pm Welcome and hymn
6.35 pm Description of Alpha and one or two testi-
         monies from people who have just completed
         the last course. We would suggest that nothing
         else is promoted at this point.
6.45 pm Prayers – short and looking out to the wider
         world, rather than for the guests at the service
6.50 pm Praise and worship
7.05 pm Sermon – evangelistic and challenging
         Opportunity to say a prayer along the lines of
         Why Jesus? p20
7.35 pm Hymn or song
7.40 pm Final prayer, blessing and offer of one-to-one
         prayer ministry

Other churches have found that an advertisement in the parish magazine is helpful. Another idea is to send personal invitations to people in your area.

Placing guests in groups

Often you will have very little information about your guests. From the application form you may only have their name, address, telephone number, an idea of their age and their hand-writing!

Remember that these are individuals. At Holy Trinity we pray over almost every single application and ask for guidance. If someone is not happy in their group, they might well not come back, so it is very important to get it right. If you feel there is a genuine reason (eg a large age gap from the rest of the group) why someone should move to a different group, do it in the first week otherwise it is disruptive for those in the old group as well as the new one.

If a guest is a friend of someone on the team, try to find out as much as possible about the guest which will help you to put them in the right group. Quite often, it is better not to put the guest in the same group as their friend who is helping as they often feel inhibited and unable to ask questions. Always put married couples in the same group unless specifically requested not to. Aim to arrange to do this task on the last day before the course starts. In this way last-minute applications will be on your list, allocated a group and will have a pre-printed label.

Venue

One of the features of Alpha is that the setting should be unchurchy. It can often be difficult to make a church hall look welcoming. Use standard lamps instead of over-head strip lighting; provide flowers; cover unattractive trestle tables; make sure that the room is warm but not stuffy; arrange the chairs so that guests can eat together in their groups. Make sure that there is good lighting on the speaker and that everyone is able to hear. This may involve arranging a PA system. Make sure that there is somewhere for people to leave their coats and a secure place for briefcases, bags etc.

It is also useful to have signs for directions to lavatories, the bookstall and where groups are meeting – put up a plan if necessary.

First night

Your welcoming team are going to be the first people
your guests will see. Often they arrive with many
preconceived ideas of what Christians are like, so when
they are greeted by a 'normal' person they are often
surprised and it is very important that their first
impression is a good one.

Your welcomers will need an alphabetical list of guests
with the name of their group leaders and the group
number. They will need to know how many men and
how many women are in each group. This is helpful
when unexpected guests arrive and need to be placed
very quickly in a group. Welcomers should know who
the group leaders and helpers are, and have to hand a list
and a plan of where the groups are meeting.

At the end of the first evening of the course all the
leaders and helpers should meet together to discuss and
review the evening.

Labels

Every person should have a label with their name and
group number on. (Ensure that the names are spelled

correctly – accuracy is very important.) Set up a table with labels in alphabetical order and delegate one or two people to hand them out. Give team members a different coloured label so that guests can know who they are and ask them any questions. Keep some spare labels and a list of unexpected guests so that they have a pre-prepared label for the following week. We have found it useful to continue labels until week three.

Runners

Depending on the size and venue of your course you will know at what stage you will need runners. You will need to choose a team of runners (ie those who take the guests from the door to the group) who are headed up by a strong leader. Keep a team of runners for the first three weeks. Don't use group leaders who will need to be in their groups to greet people. Again, remember that first impressions are important. The runner must be alert to remember the name, group number and location of group. The welcomer should introduce the guest to the runner who will take the guest to get a label and take them to their group and introduce them to their group leader. Then they should return quickly to the main door. Obviously, welcomers and runners should be friendly, but not effusive, as this can overwhelm guests on the first night.

Address lists

We give each group a blank form for them to fill in names and addresses and contact telephone numbers. However, it must be stressed to all the guests that this is not so that they will be sent junk mail or be chased up by telephone when they don't come back to the course. These lists are then typed up and one copy is returned to the group leader each week until the fourth week. This is so that lifts may be arranged and guests may be contacted if there is any problem. We do not give each member of the group a copy of the list – if they want to exchange addresses and telephone numbers this can be done within the group. If a guest rings the church office for a telephone number of another guest, we do not give details under any circumstances.

Bookstall

There is a list of recommended books in the Alpha manual. Ideally a bookstall should be open for the whole evening (except during the talk). Ensure that the previous weeks' talks are available on tape so that anyone who missed a session can buy the tape.

Treasurer

The treasurer will need to keep the overall accounts. He or she will also need to put out some bowls for supper money and to count it at the end of every evening. Furthermore they will need to collect and count the weekend money and the supper party money.

Worship leader

The worship leader needs to be responsible for any other

musicians, the songbooks or OHP acetates, all the sound equipment and perhaps also the taping of the talks, and will need to make sure that the weekend away has a worship leader.

Weekend administrator/organiser

Each group should fill in a form for the weekend which should be circulated two or three weeks before the event. Include on the form details of the date, price, to whom cheques should be made payable and children's rates. Ask for information regarding special diets, vegetarian meals, requests to share and late arrivals. Try to get people to arrange their own lifts and transport within the groups. Make sure that everyone has a map and a programme for the weekend (see *Practicalities*).

* Liaise with the conference centre over:
    sheets
    towels
    soap
    special diets
    bookshop – check that they are happy for you to
        take your own stock
    communion wine
    PA system
    recording equipment
    OHPs
    sports facilities
    places for small groups to meet

* Arrange for someone to look after any children (encourage people to bring their children if they would like to).
* Arrange for someone to organise entertainment on the Saturday evening.
* Arrange for someone to organise sport or other events on Saturday afternoon.

* Arrange for counsellors for people to chat to on Saturday afternoon.
* Remember to take a calculator.
* Remember to take songbooks.
* Remind guests to bring their Alpha manual and their Bible and any sports equipment.
* Take spare Bibles and manuals.
* Remember to take baskets or bowls for the collection on Sunday morning for the bursary fund.
* Keep an up-to-date list of those coming and who has paid and who has not.
* Try to keep the price under £50. Alpha weekends often fill a conference centre and you are therefore in a strong position to negotiate a good price. See the *UK Christian Handbook* (published by the Christian Research Association) for a list of conference centres.
* For those who are unable to afford the full amount, ask them to pay whatever they feel they can afford. The collection on Sunday almost always covers the amount needed.
* Remember to buy a small present for the staff at the conference centre.
* Make a plan of where everyone is sleeping. Many centres will offer to do this for you, but experience would suggest it is better to do it yourself.

Course supper – 7.00pm

Supper is an important aspect of Alpha. People often feel more relaxed chatting over supper. Often people have commented that the food kept them coming back to Alpha, so it is worth keeping the food to a good standard!

Depending on the numbers expected, arrange for a different group to cook supper each week. You will know when you need a caterer (approx 120 +). (Make sure you have enough paper plates and cups, coffee cups, knives, forks, tea, coffee, squash, milk, biscuits etc.)

If you don't have a task force, the group who cooked should do the washing up and clearing up. Using disposables will keep this to a minimum.

If a group is doing the cooking, the cost can usually be kept to approximately £1.50 per head. Put out bowls at the serving points and reimburse whoever paid for the food. If you have a caterer, we suggest a charge of approximately £2.50 or ask people to pay whatever they feel they can afford. Some suggestions for Alpha meals would include simple pasta dishes, shepherds pie, chili con carne and pizza. Make sure you have a vegetarian alternative. Many recipes can be found in *The Alpha Cookbook*.

Task force

The purpose of the Alpha task force is to provide practical services for the Alpha course. In this way very few people from the course will be asked to help with the more mundane tasks and will therefore not be distracted from their enjoyment of Alpha. The task force is vital to ensure that the course will run smoothly. They should be welcome to listen to the talks and should be given as much encouragement as possible. Always cherish your task force! A key appointment is the task force

co-ordinator, who allocates the different tasks and takes
pastoral care of the team.

The task force should make sure that enough Bibles
and manuals are available and are ready to be handed
out if necessary. Every guest should have a free manual.
Place a pile of Bibles under one of the chairs in the small
group. In this way, guests are not daunted by seeing
Bibles on every chair (at Holy Trinity, the NIV is used).
The task force should be available to help with car-
parking – an important job. (Don't forget that at the
beginning of the course, those helping with the car park
are the first people the guests will meet.) They also need
to ensure that each group has enough chairs and that
each group has a sign to identify itself. They should make
sure there are spare chairs for latecomers and then at the
end of the evening their job is to put away chairs.
Furthermore, the task force should put on any urns or
kettles and set up the coffee stations. Make sure that
every member of the task force has a name badge.

The task force should also run a bookstall, displaying
the books recommended in the Alpha Manual. These
books are available through the Alpha stockist scheme
operating in many Christian bookshops in the UK. Course
leaders might find it helpful to become Book Agents,
thereby qualifying for a discount on Alpha materials.

Alpha supper parties

For your first Alpha course, hold a supper party before
the course starts, then hold one at the end of every
course so that guests on the course can invite their
friends. Appoint one person to co-ordinate and organise
the supper party and print some attractive invitations.
These should be available at week seven for guests to
take to give to their friends. At the same time start
collecting money for the parties. Everyone should pay

for their guests as well as for themselves. Get a team together to set up the party and another for washing up and clearing up at the end. These should preferably be those who are not inviting friends. Do everything possible to create a good atmosphere. Make a table plan and try to use proper plates and glasses, etc. Put flowers, candles and napkins on the table. The talk should come during coffee.

Questionnaires

At week nine, give each guest on the course a questionnaire (see Appendix D). This will enable you to see what God has been doing in people's lives, and will help in planning the next course. At the same time, give the group leaders a questionnaire and ask them to fill in details about every single member of their group (take the names from the address lists even if guests have not completed the course). Ask them whether their group members completed the course and, if not, do they know the reason. Ask them if their group members are going to do *A Life Worth Living* and then whether they are going into a home group (ask them to specify which one). Bearing in mind the supper party and perhaps the guest service before the next course, ask who could give a good testimony. Ask who would be a good Alpha helper, and make sure that you remember to invite them to help on the next course.

Philippa Pearson Miles was the administrator of the Holy Trinity Brompton evening Alpha course from 1992 to 1996.

anything else?

Appendix C
Daytime Courses
by Deidre Hurst

Daytime Alpha is held on Wednesday mornings and was originally designed for those who were likely to find it easier to attend a course during the day rather than in the evening. There are obvious categories: people with young children, those who are self-employed or unemployed and those who would prefer not to venture out alone at night. In our experience this has generally been a group for women, but lately, we have successfully included one or two men.

The daytime Alpha course has proved as successful as the evening course as a means of evangelism. This course, with its appeal to both the head and the heart, has seen many people come into relationship with Christ – from those very far away from Christianity to those who have sat in pews in churches for much of their lives, but have not understood that the heart of the Christian faith is a relationship with Jesus. One team member, who had brought about twelve people from her own church to do the morning course at Holy Trinity Brompton, said to me at the end of the ten weeks that she had sat for years in the church with these people and none of them had moved in any real way towards conversion. Now, many had been converted during the course and they all wanted to go on to another Alpha course.

Values

The daytime Alpha course promotes the same values as the evening Alpha with some small differences of emphasis, resulting from the time of day we meet and particularly from the ministry of 'women to women'.

Anyone may come, at any stage of their life and from any background. As with the evening Alpha it is very important to make people feel welcome. We try to foster relationships in a relaxed atmosphere. Although we only have one lunch together as part of the course, it is very often a sign of the groups gelling together and friendships being formed when groups begin to arrange to have lunch together after the course is over.

Many women these days do some kind of course in the morning – art, history, languages etc – so we can encourage them to come and learn about the Christian faith. We also find that many, even those who are not Christians, have been crying out to God for their needs and those of their family (without knowing him or his power to change things). As a consequence, they readily understand about prayer and begin to pray together early in the course.

Choosing the team and the helpers

We have the same priorities as for an evening Alpha; choosing people who have vision for what the course can do and choosing new Christians who have a lot of friends who do not know Christ and training them to be helpers for the next course. We find it possible to have smaller groups with the daytime Alpha, maybe eight or even six and we have two team members and one helper to each group.

Groups

Most tend to enjoy the groups more than anything else. They often come needing love, acceptance and forgiveness and they find it in their groups. Some come with damaged lives from abuse of all kinds. Many need a place of peace where they can learn to accept God's forgiveness for those things they have done of which they feel ashamed, and where they can learn to trust God and to forgive those who have hurt them. We try to put people of similar age together and possibly those who live near each other. We find in particular that mothers enjoy being with others who have children of a similar age, as it means they all have similar joys and problems.

Setting for daytime Alpha

As with evening Alpha, daytime Alpha probably works best meeting in a home but can work very well in a church hall or similar building, providing there is room for a creche.

Numbers

The course seems to work equally well whatever the numbers. We have done courses from twenty people to two hundred with the Lord working in equal power in people's lives.

Resources

You will need one copy of the Alpha manual and some

training manuals for the team. The training manual, although geared for an evening Alpha, can be used equally well for a morning Alpha, disregarding only Appendix III, which is concerned with evening timings. If you prefer to do the course by listening to the tapes then these can be supplied. There is also a talk geared specially to women, 'What is special about the Christian family?', with notes available from Holy Trinity Brompton.

Task force

It is important to be well organised and to have someone from among the helpers who will organise the coffee for each morning, set out chairs, organise the creche and be responsible for arranging the lunch. There should also be a prayer task force from the team, who meet together for prayer half an hour before the morning begins. All the team will be committed to praying but with the timing of school runs and other morning commitments, it is not always possible for all the team to meet beforehand.

Invitations and timing

We suggest a letter or invitation card inviting people to join the morning Alpha course, telling them how long the course is to run and the timing of the morning. For example:

MORNING ALPHA
29th September - 8th December
We invite you to join the new
Morning Alpha course
beginning on
29th September

The course runs for ten weeks on a Wednesday morning at _____ from 10.00 am to 12 noon approx. The mornings provide time for a talk on Christian basics, followed by a break for coffee, then discussion groups, with an opportunity to ask questions. There will be a special half-day with lunch on 10th November when the talk will be 'How can I be filled with the Holy Spirit?' – further details later.

The course is ideal for anyone who wants to learn more about the Christian faith and/or anyone who would like to enquire into what Christianity really means. It is a wonderful opportunity to meet new people and make new friends. There are creche facilities if you need them.

Timing

The timing for the mornings works as follows:

10.05 am	Welcome
	Worship
10.15	Notices
10.20 (approx)	Talk
11.00	Coffee break
11.20 (approx)	Groups
12.00	Creche ends

The main difference in the organisation and timing is the absence of the weekend away as we feel on the whole it is not practical for women to be separated from their families at the weekend. So instead we have a day beginning with coffee at 10 o'clock, followed by worship and a talk on 'How can I be filled with the Spirit?' Then we have ministry followed by lunch. After lunch there is an opportunity to get into the groups for questions or more prayer. This finishes at about 2.30 pm in good time for school runs.

Daytime Alpha supper

The supper party at the end of the course is an excellent setting for married women to bring their husbands who, as we have found many times, have been very pleasantly surprised at some of the changes in the lives of their spouses, and it gives them a wonderful opportunity to hear the gospel in a relaxed environment. It has been one of the striking features of daytime Alpha that many of the husbands have gone on to do an evening Alpha and been converted to Christ. Of course, we do have many women on the course who are not married and they are more than welcome to bring their friends to the supper party.

The results of daytime Alpha

During the seven years that we have had a daytime Alpha, we have had many wonderful conversions and healings. We have often found that after only a few weeks of the course whole families are coming to church.

Deidre Hurst has been running daytime Alpha at Holy Trinity Brompton for seven years as well as leading Alpha courses in other parts of the country.

Appendix D
Questionnaire

Name

Group

1. How did you hear about the Alpha course? Did you come to an Alpha supper party?

2. Why did you decide to do Alpha?

3. How many sessions did you attend?

4. (a) (i) Were you a Christian when you started the course?
    (ii) Were you a regular churchgoer when you started the course?

    (b) How would you describe yourself now (in terms of the Christian faith)?

    (c) If the answer to (a) and (b) is different, when and how did the change occur?

5. In what ways, if any, did you benefit from doing the Alpha course?

6. What did you enjoy most about Alpha?

7. What did you find most difficult?

8. (a) Which, if any, tapes did you buy?

   (b) Which, if any, books did you buy?

   (c) Did you find them helpful and if so why?
   (please name any books or tapes which you found particularly helpful)

9. In what way could the course be improved?

   (a)   Talks

   (b)   Small groups

   (c)   Generally

10. Any other comments

Appendix E
What Course Leaders say about Alpha

'I've been involved in full time, front line evangelism for the past decade, both nationally and at local church level. I have never found a more significant tool for my trade than Alpha.'

Duncan Banks
Banbury Baptist Church, Oxon

'...this evangelist can confidently say that it is the most effective form of evangelism and nurture he's ever experienced – and anyone can do it.'

Paul Hamilton
St Paul's, Hainault, Essex

'I firmly believe Alpha is a real gift from the Lord for this church at this time.'

Chris Halliwell
The Wrentham Benefice, Suffolk

'...a major influence on the evangelistic strategy for local churches in the UK at this time.'

Peter Stott
Havant Community Church, Bedhampton

'I think Alpha could form a very valuable role in the Catholic church.'

Michael Aust
Diocese of Arundel and Brighton

'The videos are absolutely brilliant. They are basic, straightforward, and easily accessible to everybody ... We are making Alpha central in the life of the church – not just a fringe activity.'

Ann Douglas
Vicar of All Saints, Oxhey

'The sceptics among us are now hanging our heads in shame. Alpha has proved a valuable teaching and evangelistic tool in Hong Kong and has already been instrumental in changing lives and bringing people to Christ.'

Steve Miller
Union Church, Hong Kong

'With no one else to guide us, we simply followed each step of *Telling Others* and were wonderfully pleased with the results. For some it was their first "live encounter" with God.'

Brian McVitty
St Paul's on the Hill Church, Toronto, Canada

'This has been the most successful soul-winning campaign that we have seen for a long time.'

R. J. Lillyman
St Paul's Church, Worcester

'People are rallying round and getting excited about seeing God work.'

R. Banks
Protestant Cathedral of the Holy Trinity, Brussels, Belgium

'We feel a key to this whole vision of how to get Asians to make that decision for Christ is the Alpha course.'

Pall Singh
Solihull Christian Fellowship

'Alpha has given new enthusiasm to the whole church. Many are taking non-Christian friends along to Alpha.'

M. Lange
Bergen Alpha, Norway

'A wonderful and very effective tool for communicating the basics of orthodox Catholic faith in an ordinary non-eclectic parish. Yes, it is hard work, but it's well worth the effort.'

Bryan Hackney
Vicar of St Francis Church, Mackworth Estate, Derby

'Alpha is quite the most exciting thing I have done in over forty years as a Christian.'

Andrew Bentley-Taylor
Ledbury, Herefordshire

'If people say Alpha doesn't work in the inner city it just shows that people haven't tried it. Often, I think, it is said by people who are theorists working from the outside and not by practitioners who have tried it on the inside. Those of us who've done it in the inner city are the people who can say, "Actually, we know it works."'

Eric Delve
Vicar, St Lawrence Church, Liverpool

'Alpha has had a profound effect on the lives of the people at our churches.'

Christopher Simms
Parish of St Michael, Stanwix with St Mark, Belah, Carlisle

'We have seen a huge change in these guys over the months they have been at the SAFE and doing the Alpha course.'

SAFE, a homeless project based at St James the Less Church in Pimlico

'People have been strengthened in their faith, others converted and filled with the Spirit.'

W. G. Wood
St Mary, Surrey

'Time and again it seems the Alpha course is tailor-made for each person attending.'

Charles Fox
St Kea, Truro

'Alpha has given a sense of mission and purpose, and that we really are "doing evangelism" as a church. It has stretched several church members who have been able leaders or helpers.'

Chris Oldroyd
Riverside Church, Farnham, Surrey

'Overall, the course induced within us an internal joy that we were anxious to share with each other, and a wider desire to share that experience with our families, friends and colleagues.'

Reba Longhorn
St Mary's Roman Catholic Church, Woburn Sands

'It has been an experience and an adventure … It has opened up new horizons before us.'

Roy Humphries
Dunfermline

'…it has revitalised the church.'

S. McLean
Ammanford Evangelical Church, Dyfed, Wales

'People have discovered Spirit-filled life for the first time. There is a fresh approach to worship and service.'

Trevor Green
North East Tameside Alpha, Cheshire

'Alpha has given the congregation a sense of direction and purpose.'

R. Sanderson
Shawlands Cross Church, Glasgow

'Forty-two converted during Alpha, twenty-one new Christians followed up through Alpha and eight returned to Christ. A course that has encouraged the church.'

A. Mackie
Riverside, Birmingham

'Alpha has brought people to faith, opened them to the fullness of the Spirit, given them a love for the Bible and deepened their understanding of and relationship to God.'

R. Simpson
St Mary's, Gloucestershire

'The fellowship that has been generated during Alpha has spread over into the church and people are noticing something wonderful has really happened.'

L. Ling
North Walsham Methodist, Norfolk

'The inmates are now praying together in the small groups which is very moving to see. The prison officers can tell that they have changed.'

Peter Lockyer
Chaplaincy team member, Young Offender Institution, Glen Parva, Wigston, Leicestershire

'My doubts as to whether something that obviously worked in a large urban church – where young people predominate – would transfer to a small rural situation with a much higher average age, were completely unfounded.'

Roy Eames
Colwall Free Church, Herefordshire

'It has brought strategy into evangelism. It has helped people understand more of the "process" of salvation.'

D. Wuyts
Gosbecks Christian Fellowship, Colchester, Essex

'Existing members have been renewed and revitalised. New people have come to faith and joined the church. It is helping the church turn around to be more mission-minded.'

Mike Watson
St Alkmunds, Derby

'Alpha has helped to bring renewal, put evangelism at the

heart of the church, and increase our evangelism effectiveness.'

Charles Croll
Plume Avenue URC, Colchester, Essex

'Alpha has provided a focus for evangelism in a sustainable programme. We have had twenty-five new converts who are in church on Sundays.'

Tim Humphrey
Springfield Church, Wallington, Surrey

'The Alpha course has drawn us together, given us a greater passion for evangelism and most importantly drawn us closer to Jesus.'

M. Cooper
Hampton Baptist Church, Middlesex

'Alpha has led members from being churchgoers to being Spirit-filled Christians.'

Jean Lupton
Long Eaton Churches Fellowship, Derbyshire

'Alpha is something the folk here have been able to relate to. We have seen God's power moving; we have seen the Holy Spirit work in lives; and we have seen people converted.'

Lance Cavan
Christchurch, Eston, Teesside

'The Alpha course came at the right time. Personally, I don't think there is a lot of adaptation needed because I think it's so easy to understand. Basically we're following the book and the tapes very closely and it works.'

Bill Sanders
Vicar of St Bridge's, a UPA parish on the borders of Toxteth,
Liverpool

Appendix F
Common Questions

Is there a pattern emerging for numbers on an Alpha course?

As we have listened to feedback from various churches over the last three years patterns are beginning to emerge.

The first course

One way to start is simply to begin with a small group of anyone interested and allow it to grow from there. Another way is to start by introducing Alpha to the whole church. The advantage of this is that:

- Everyone in the church can see what Alpha is and how it works. Hopefully this will build confidence in the course.
- Alpha may act as a programme of renewal for the church.

However, it needs to be borne in mind that there are two possible disadvantages:

- Those from the fringe of the church and beyond are less likely to feel at home on a course which is predominantly church members.
- There could be a sense of anti-climax as the second course may be smaller than the first.

Subsequent courses

Where the first course has been run for the whole church

191

there tends to be a sharp drop in numbers for the second course. For example, the first course might have 50-100 people on it.

By the time the second course starts, most church members will have already done the course. Thus the second course may be very small – possibly five or six people. It is important that the church is not discouraged by this. It is likely that this small group will include fringe members or even outsiders. Thus the course is beginning to fulfil its function, ie to draw in those outside the church.

Hopefully, if one or two of those come to Christ and are filled with the Spirit they will become excited about Jesus and bring along their family and friends. So, the third course will be slightly bigger. Numbers might look something like this:

First course   50-100
Second course   10-15
Third course   15-20
Fourth course   20-25

It is important to remember that ideally Alpha is a rolling programme of evangelism. It may take a few courses to iron out the difficulties in getting started and for church members to gain the confidence to invite their friends.

The important thing is not to be discouraged if initially there is a drop in numbers. At this stage perseverance is required. For it is only as outsiders are attracted to the church that the real purpose of Alpha is starting to be fulfilled.

What does Alpha teach about the sacraments?

The Alpha course includes material on the sacraments of baptism and Holy Communion. This can be found in Chapter 14 of *Questions of Life* ('What about the Church?'). Teaching on Holy Communion is given in the context of an informal Communion service on the Sunday morning of the weekend away. (It is not, for that reason, included on the video or audio tapes.)

Alpha is now being run by all the major denominations in the UK and is endorsed by Christian leaders across the traditions. Teaching on the sacraments is limited, in the sense that we only teach on Alpha what all the major denominations and traditions are agreed about. For example, we teach about the essential meaning and necessity of baptism but we do not go into the divisive issue of infant baptism.

We encourage all new Christians who have not been baptised to be baptised at the end of the course. In our particular church, which is an Anglican one, we do practise infant baptism because we believe it is the biblical pattern and the traditional practice of the church down the ages. We do not re-baptise those who have already been baptised as infants. However, we recognise that many Christians, especially those of Baptist, Pentecostal and Neo-Pentecostal backgrounds do not accept this as the biblical norm or the historical practice of the church. So we refrain from teaching this on Alpha and ask the other denominations to exercise a similar degree of restraint.

This enables us all to teach the same material. It means that people can recommend Alpha courses in any part of the country to their friends and family, without checking the theological position of those teaching the course to ensure it accords with their own.

In the case of the teaching on Holy Communion, again we try to teach what all the major denominations agree about. We are aware that some denominations and traditions would like to add more. Again, we ask them to refrain from doing so during the Alpha course. But they are, of course, free to do so afterwards in their own church membership courses.

As an Anglican church we would teach our own views in our confirmation classes. Others – for example, Roman Catholics or Baptists – might teach something different.

This would not form part of the course itself.

So, although the teaching on the sacraments is limited on the course itself, both the teaching and the practice of the sacraments of baptism and Holy Communion form an essential part of the course.

Appendix G
Alpha Copyright Statement

Sandy Millar, Vicar of Holy Trinity Brompton, writes:

> We have always been keen to allow individuals who are
> running an Alpha course the flexibility to adapt where it was
> felt necessary to allow for locally felt needs and where there
> was the desire to retain the essential elements, nature and
> identity of the course. Experience has shown though that this
> has been misunderstood and the resulting loss of integrity in
> some courses has given rise to considerable confusion. Now
> that Alpha is running all around the world we have
> reluctantly had to draw up a tighter copyright statement in
> order to preserve confidence and quality control. I am sure
> you will understand.

(i) With the exception of books published by Kingsway (in
     which the author is stated to hold the copyright), all
     Alpha resources and materials, including booklets,
     tapes and graphics, are copyright to Holy Trinity
     Brompton.
(ii) In no circumstances may any part of any Alpha
     resource be reproduced or transmitted in any form or
     by any means, electronic or mechanical, including
     photocopying, recording, or any information storage
     and retrieval system, without permission in writing
     from the copyright holder or that holder's agent.
(iii) Use of Alpha resources is permitted only when in
     conjunction with the running or promotion of an Alpha
     course. Resale, or the obtaining of payment in any other

connection with any Alpha resource is not permitted.
(iv) Holy Trinity Brompton asks that the name 'Alpha', or names similar to it, should not be used in connection with any other Christian course. This request is made in order to:

– avoid confusion caused by different courses having similar titles;

– ensure the uniformity and integrity of the Alpha course; and

– to maintain confidence in courses listed on the Alpha register.

(v) Holy Trinity Brompton will allow minor adaptations to be made to the Alpha course in the following situation and manner:

(a) The Alpha course may be altered as stated below, provided that the person developing the altered version neither uses nor promotes such a course outside his or her home church or parish. No other person may so use or promote such a course. The altered course must be used only in the church or parish of the person who developed it.

(b) (i) Subject to (ii) below, the Alpha course may be shortened or lengthened by varying the length of the talks or the number of sessions. Not all the material need be used; additional material may be used.

(ii) Such alterations must not change the essential character of the course. Alpha is a series of about fifteen talks, given over a period of time, including a weekend or day away, with teaching based on the material in *Questions of Life*.

This statement supersedes all previous statements relating to copyright in any Alpha resource.

2 October 1996

Appendix H
Alpha Resources

1. What do we need to run an Alpha course?

Questions of Life with Study Guide by Nicky Gumbel (published by Kingsway). This book contains the fifteen talks from the Alpha course in written form and is a primary resource. It is useful for church leaders preparing material for their Alpha talks. Course leaders and helpers will find it useful for reference during the course.

Participants on Alpha are encouraged to read *Questions of Life* at some point on the course to reinforce what they are learning. It is an ideal book to give to anyone interested in the Christian faith.

The Alpha Manual (published by HTB Publications). Each guest on the course receives a copy of the manual. The manual contains an outline of each of the fifteen talks, including Scripture references, enabling guests to follow the teaching more easily and to make notes. Also it leaves them with a record of the course material to keep.

The Alpha course on video (published by HTB Publications). The fifteen Alpha course talks on five videos, presented by Nicky Gumbel at Holy Trinity Brompton. Each video features three of the Alpha talks and each talk runs for approximately one hour. Many Alpha leaders have used them to run the Alpha course where there is no obvious leader, and over a third of all courses in the UK are now using the videos.

The Alpha course on cassette (published by HTB Publications). The fifteen Alpha course talks given by Nicky Gumbel on cassette. Some Alpha course leaders have run the course using the tapes and it is also a useful aid for those preparing to lead or help with groups on the Alpha course. In addition, it is easy to give course participants a tape to listen to if they miss one of the Alpha talks.

Why Jesus? by Nicky Gumbel (published by Kingsway). This is a short evangelistic booklet, full of contemporary illustrations.

Alpha course leaders may wish to give the booklet to guests who come to the Alpha supper or Sunday guest services, or indeed anyone who asks, 'What is the point of Christianity?'

Why Christmas? is the Christmas edition of *Why Jesus?* and makes an ideal Christmas gift.

The Alpha Youth Manual (11-14s) (published by HTB Publications). This manual is designed to appeal to a younger audience, with fun illustrations and thought provoking text. Designed by Kristy Giddy.

The *Youth Alpha Manual (15-18s)* (published by HTB Publications). This manual is designed to appeal to an older youth audience and is compiled by the Revd Simon Jones who has much experience in running youth Alpha.

The Youth Alpha Leader's Manual (published by HTB Publications). Designed to equip youth leaders to run Alpha in their church, school or with any group of young people. Full of inspirational ideas and guidance for those wishing to lead a youth Alpha group.

2. What do we need to train the team?

The Alpha Team Training Video (published by HTB

Publications). The three-session training course including talks on 'Leading small groups', 'Pastoral care' and 'Ministry'. Presented by Nicky Gumbel at Holy Trinity Brompton, this course is designed to equip Alpha leaders and helpers to run their small groups effectively.

The Alpha Team Training Tapes (published by HTB Publications). The three-session training course for Alpha leaders and helpers on cassette.

The Alpha Team Training Manual (published by HTB Publications). To be given to each Alpha leader and helper to complement the training. Printed with space to write notes.

Searching Issues with Study Guide (published by Kingsway). This book tackles the seven issues most often raised on Alpha and provides invaluable help to those struggling with questions like, 'Why does God allow suffering?' and 'Is there anything wrong with sex before marriage?' Alpha leaders and helpers will find *Searching Issues* useful as they prepare for the Alpha course. It is an ideal book to give to friends or those interested in straight answers to tough questions about Christianity.

3. What do we need to introduce Alpha to our church?

Alpha Introductory video (published by HTB Publications). A fifteen-minute promotional video to give an introduction to the Alpha course. Ideal for those wishing to find out more about Alpha. It answers questions such as 'What is Alpha?', 'Who is it for?' and 'How does it work?'.

How to run the Alpha course (video) (published by HTB Publications). This video focuses on the principles and practicalities of running Alpha. Contains video notes. Ideal for those wanting to set up Alpha in their church.

How to run the Alpha course (cassette) (published by HTB

Publications). Twelve tapes on how to run an Alpha course. Contains the two main sessions on the principles and practicalities of running Alpha as well as talks on 'Worship on Alpha', 'Ministry on Alpha', 'Daytime Alpha' and 'Youth Alpha' among others.

Alpha Worship (published by HTB Publications). A comprehensive training resource for those wishing to introduce worship on the Alpha course. Specifically designed for Alpha course leaders, worship leaders and music teams, as well as small groups who wish to worship without live accompaniment. Contains a 16-track CD or cassette, a manual, teaching tape and songbook.

4. What do we need for follow-up after Alpha?

A Life Worth Living with Study Guide (published by Kingsway). This book was specifically written to be a follow-up to the Alpha course. The nine chapters make up nine Bible studies based on the letter to the Philippians. The aim of the book is to introduce, in a simple and practical way, a key letter in the New Testament to those who are just starting in the Christian life and beginning to read the Bible.

A Life Worth Living cassette and manual (published by HTB Publications). Extremely useful for small groups or home groups to use to study together as follow-up material to Alpha.

Searching Issues with Study Guide (published by Kingsway). As already mentioned this book tackles the seven issues most often raised on Alpha. It is also recommended as a post-Alpha course and can be used in conjunction with the tapes and manual listed below.

Searching Issues cassette and manual (published by HTB Publications). Again, extremely useful for use in small groups or home groups as follow-up material to Alpha.

Challenging Lifestyle with Study Guide (published by Kingsway). This book is designed to be part of a range of post-Alpha products for new Christians. Based on the Sermon on the Mount this book demonstrates how Jesus' teaching not only challenges our contemporary lifestyle but presents us with a radical alternative that is in every sense the 'ultimate challenge'. This book contains nineteen chapters and could cover two terms of teaching.

Challenging Lifestyle cassette and manual (published by HTB Publications). Again, extremely useful to use in small groups or home groups as follow-up material to Alpha.

5. What do we need to promote Alpha in our church?

Alpha News is the newspaper published by HTB Publications and mailed to all those promoting the Alpha course in their local church. It is available free from STL. It comes out three times a year and is designed to equip those setting up and running Alpha courses. It features 'What is Alpha?' with a step-by-step outline of how to run the Alpha course. It also contains the Alpha register (a list of courses running, both nationwide and internationally) and testimonies of people who have run a course, or participated in one.

The Alpha poster pack (published by HTB Publications). Two different sizes. One pack contains an A3, an A2 and two A4 posters. The second pack contains two A1 posters in four-colour, ideal for promoting the Alpha course or the Alpha product range. Alpha car stickers are also available.

Alpha brochures. Customised brochures are available direct from the Alpha office. A four-colour brochure, ideal for promoting your Alpha course, containing an application form and your church details printed by us. These are also available, with blank spaces for overprinting, in packs of 100 from the Alpha hotline.

All Kingsway books are available through your local
Christian bookshops or from Kingsway Publications,
Lottbridge Drove, Eastbourne, East Sussex BN23 6NT
(Freephone 0800 525984). The additional Alpha resources
are published by HTB Publications. Alpha resources are
also available from your local Christian bookshop or
through STL, PO Box 300, Kingstown Broadway, Carlisle,
Cumbria CA3 0QS. For more information contact the Alpha
Office at Holy Trinity Brompton (Telephone 0171 581 8255,
Fax 0171 584 8536, e-mail htb.london@dial.pipex.com).

Alpha **Hotline for telephone orders:**
0345 581278 (all calls at local rate)

Notes

1. Statistics from *1992 Social Trends* from the Central Statistical Office.

2. Leading missiologist David Bosch defines evangelism as the proclamation of salvation in Christ to those who do not believe in him, calling them to repentance and conversion, announcing forgiveness of sin, inviting them to become living members of Christ's earthly community and to begin a life of service to others in the power of the Holy Spirit.

3. John Stott, *The Contemporary Christian* (IVP, 1992), p241.

4. Michael Green, *Evangelism through the Local Church* (Hodder & Stoughton, 1990), pix.

5. John Stott, *The Contemporary Christian* (IVP, 1992), pp121, 127.

6. Graham Tomlin, *Evangelical Anglicans* ed R. T. France and A. E. McGrath (SPCK, 1993), pp82-95.

7. John Stott, *Issues Facing Christians Today* (Marshalls, 1984), pxi.

8. Lesslie Newbigin, *The Open Secret* (SPCK, 1995), p11.

9. Wayne Grudem, *Systematic Theology* (IVP, 1994), pp763-787.

10. David Pawson, *Fourth Wave* (Hodder & Stoughton, 1993), pp36-37.

11. John Pollock, *John Wesley* (Hodder & Stoughton, 1989), p118.

12. George Whitefield's *Journal* (Banner of Truth, 1992).

13. Charles Finney, *Memoirs of Rev. Charles G. Finney* (New York: Fleming H. Revell, 1876), p19.

14. John Pollock, *Moody without Sankey* (Hodder & Stoughton, 1963), pp83, 87.

15. R. A. Torrey, *The Baptism with the Holy Spirit* (Dimension Books, 1972), pp11, 54.

16. John Pollock, *Billy Graham* (Hodder & Stoughton, 1966), pp62-63.

17. Nicky Gumbel, *Questions of Life* (Kingsway, 1993).

18. Nicky Gumbel, *Why Jesus?* (Kingsway, 1991).

19. Juan Carlos Ortiz, quoted in *Alpha* Magazine, January 1993.

20. R. A. Torrey, *Personal Work* (Pickering & Inglis, 1974), pp9-10.

21. Nicky Gumbel, *Searching Issues* (Kingsway, 1994).

22. *Church Times*, 7th September 1989.

23. C. H. Spurgeon, *Lectures to My Students* (Marshall Pickering, 1954), p77.

24. Phillips Brooks, *Lectures on Preaching: The Yale Lectures* (Dutton, 1877; Allenson, 1895; Baker, 1969), p28.

25. The New Bible Dictionary (InterVarsity Press, 1962), p827.

Alpha

This book is an Alpha resource. The Alpha course is a practical introduction to the Christian faith initiated by Holy Trinity Brompton in London, and now being run by thousands of churches throughout the UK as well as overseas.

For more information on Alpha, and details of tapes, videos and training manuals, contact the Alpha office, Holy Trinity Brompton on 0171-581 8255, or STL, PO Box 300, Kingstown Broadway, Carlisle, Cumbria CA3 0QS.

All the books are available from your local Christian bookshop, or through Kingsway Publications, Lottbridge Drove, Eastbourne, E. Sussex BN23 6NT (Freephone 0800 378446).

Alpha Hotline for telephone orders:
0345 581278 (all calls at local rate)

 Kingsway Publications

 Alpha